curse of
the mommy

curse of the mommy

pregnant thoughts
and postpartum impressions
of a reluctant mom

cathy crimmins

A PERIGEE BOOK

Perigee Books
are published by
The Putnam Publishing Group
200 Madison Avenue
New York, NY 10016

The author gratefully acknowledges permission to reprint the following:
Illustration on page 73 from *It's a Mom's Life*, by David Sipress.
Copyright © 1988 by David Sipress. Used by permission of New American
Library, a division of Penguin Books USA, Inc. Illustrations on pages
21, 50, 97, 115, 123, from *It's Still a Mom's Life*, by David Sipress.
Copyright © 1993 by David Sipress. Used by permission of New
American Library, a division of Penguin Books USA, Inc.

Library of Congress Cataloging-in-Publication Data

Crimmins, C. E.
Curse of the mommy : pregnant thoughts and postpartum impressions
of a reluctant mom / Cathy Crimmins.
ISBN 0-399-51819-3
p.   cm.
1. Pregnancy—Humor.   2. Motherhood—Humor.   I. Title.
RG121.C85   1993   92-44746 CIP
618.2'00207—dc20

Cover illustration © 1993 by Lisa Goldrick
Printed in the United States of America
1 2 3 4 5 6 7 8 9 10

This book is printed on acid-free paper.

To Alan and Kelly

I'd like to thank my extended dysfunctional family for bothering and encouraging me: Larry Balick, Louise Berliner, Barbara Blake, Frank Costello, Sloan Harris, Marsha Gerdes, Nick Kulish, Betty Lancaster, Sandy Masayko, Kate Maskar, Wendy Nelson, Flash Rosenberg, Sally Schreiber, Bruce Schimmel, Robin Warshaw, and Ivana Willis. Honorable mention goes to Tom Maeder and St. James Shatzer for brainstorming assistance far beyond the call of duty. Thanks also to the kind folks at Trinity Playgroup, who try to give my child the normal upbringing she deserves.

My life could not have been lived and this book could not have been written without Alan Forman, beloved sperm donor and decorated veteran of domestic battles. Writers are weird people, and I'm sorry he had to marry one. But at least he's not related to me by blood, as is my poor daughter. Thanks, Kelly—the therapy's on me.

My emotional debts continue to mount. Kelly's sisters, Sarah and Joanne Babaian, persist in adoring my child. Joellen Brown persists in believing in my career. Jon Winokur brought out the curmudgeon in me and supplied many a pep talk. Steve Ross made a good labor coach, while Lisa Bankoff acted as literary midwife to ensure speedy delivery. Thank you, everybody.

contents

PART I

the parasite

(From Conception to Birth)

PART II

bootie camp

PART III

terror in tinytown

➤➤➤➤➤➤➤➤

PART I

the parasite

From conception to labor and birth,
that goshdarn Miracle of Life . . .

the making of an anti-mom

Flashback: A Christmas Party, ca. 1970.

Enter a fifteen-year-old girl in a mangy mouton coat. Laughing, oblivious, she throws her coat on top of a baby fast asleep on a couch.

Cut to: Mother of baby, coming back into the room and becoming frantic when she cannot locate her infant. She gasps as she spies the outline of her offspring under five pounds of smelly lambskin.

"Who did that?" screams the mother, as all eyes follow the teenaged girl scurrying toward the door.

I was that careless girl, and this adolescent episode was my last physical contact with a human baby until eighteen years later when my daughter popped out. I had never held an infant or tried to put a sock onto someone else's foot or even realized that there was a whole population of subhumans out there incapable of using the toilet or reading a newspaper. At least when I finally met my own baby, I wasn't wearing a coat, and I was in too much pain to remain completely oblivious to her presence.

But this incident should have told me something about my maternal instincts. Aren't girls supposed to have some sort of radar for babies? If so, mine didn't improve with age. After Kelly was born, I frequently misplaced her around the house. I would leave her on the kitchen counter snoozing in her little baby bucket and then go away. Later I'd look for her in the living room, and only when I noticed that she wasn't there would I retrace my steps to find her, sort of like the way I hunt for my keys.

Nature has its ways of compensating for the motherhood-impaired, so the little ecosystem surrounding me eventually took over. My cats figured out pretty quickly that they could use this new hairless feline

13

to get more food. They'd wake her up, get her crying to attract my attention, and only then would I find out where she was. I only wish they had also taught her how to use the litter box.

Yep—I should have known in my teenaged years that motherhood was not a job for people who don't notice animate objects lurking on couches. But I never really thought about it much. Logically, cynics and airheads like myself should represent some dead end of the human race and be unable to breed. I slipped through the evolutionary net and became a mom anyway. And the deeper I fall under the spell of the Curse of the Mommy, the more I realize that there's no reason that parenthood should be restricted to people who actually like children.

What is an Anti-Mom? She's somebody who might have heeded her biological clock but will need another eighteen years to figure out if it was a false alarm. There's a little bit of the Anti-Mom in every mom, no matter how sweet she might seem on the surface. Every mom has an evil twin who might get kicked out of Mister Rogers's neighborhood if she vented her true feelings about para-adult lifeforms.

So, for the benefit of all Anti-Moms in and out of the closet, here's a checklist of symptoms:

An Anti-Mom

- forgets to carry Kleenex;
- cannot name all the Muppets;
- asks to be seated several rows away from her own child on airplanes;
- grows nauseous listening to Raffi songs;
- could not tell you what size shoe her kid wears if her life depended on it;
- sneers when she sees other people's children in restaurants;
- thinks "babyproofing" means contraception;
- throws her own tantrums in supermarkets;

- does her bit for saving Planet Earth by keeping her kid in the same disposable diaper for eighteen hours;
- volunteers her kid for Vasectomy Poster Child.

The Anti-Mom Hall of Fame

Morticia Addams
Joan Crawford
The Old Woman Who Lived in a Shoe
Peg Bracken
Peg Bundy
Olive Oyl
My Mother the Car
Erma Bombeck
Nora Charles
Roseanne Barr
"Fergie," Duchess of York
Female Guppies
Auntie Mame
Auntie Em
Aunt Fritzi
Ma Barker
Medea
Betty Friedan
Nora in Ibsen's *A Doll's House*
Nancy Reagan
Murphy Brown
Uncle Charlie on *My Three Sons*
George Sand
Queen Gertrude of Denmark (Hamlet's mother)
Mrs. Bates (Norman's mother)
Jocasta (Oedipus's mother)
Margaret Thatcher
Mary, Queen of Scots

Anti-Moms Without Children

Josephine the Plumber
Dorothy Parker
Madonna
Queen Elizabeth I
Leona Helmsley
Lady Macbeth
Betty Boop
Katharine Hepburn
Miss Kitty
Camille Paglia
Zsa Zsa Gabor
Emma Peel

conceptual difficulties

Even when you're trying to achieve fertility, nothing really prepares you for getting knocked up. But the least you can expect when it happens is a little romance, a little glamour.

My significant sperm donor did not rise to the occasion. Okay, so maybe I was hopelessly warped by watching too many old flicks as a kid. But I'll never forgive him for flunking the Movie Pregnancy Test.

Movie pregnancies are my ideal. Usually they skip right from the cheery, misty-eyed announcement of conception until long after the blessed event, when the kid looks like a real person instead of a bald alien.

I always imagined using as my model the way a woman announces her pregnancy in old movies. I wanted to tell my man in some wholesome yet alluring way (preferably wearing a cute negligee right after my hair had been done) that I was going to bear his child, and then watch him get all goofy and starry-eyed. I wanted him to become boyishly concerned about my pregnant fragility and tell me to sit down and then gaze into my eyes and explain how he was going to build me a home, a real home that our children and grandchildren could live in forever. And then I wanted him to blather on about how he wished our child would look exactly like me, and about how lucky he was that he ever married such a terrific woman.

Basically, I wanted a scene from *It's a Wonderful Life*. What I got was one from *Dial "M" for Murder*.

Probably it was my mistake. I wasn't mature enough to wait until my significant sperm donor came home from work. I had to call him instead, and take my advice: Phone conception is not as satisfying as phone sex.

Probably, too, you should never begin a telephone conversation by saying, "The test tube turned blue." This type of approach confuses men, who need a long time to figure out how science affects their daily lives.

When I used that laboratory-style announcement on my husband, the phone line seemed to go dead. After a while, I connected cause and effect for him. "So that means I'm pregnant."

"Geez, you're kidding. What are we going to do?"

"What do you mean, what are we going to do? I've been trying to get pregnant for over a year."

"What are we going to do?"

"Hey—what are you, seventeen? This is your wife talking. We're going to have a baby."

"Holy shit. Look, sorry, I can't deal with this now. I gotta go."

Jimmy Stewart never would have played the scene that way. Maybe Mickey Rourke. But that's not the kind of movie I want to be in.

pregnancy stages

---

1 hour

The sperm and egg have just completed their chromosomal fling—the sperm has rolled over and gone to sleep, leaving the egg to do all the work for the next nine months. If you were an amoeba you would be hanging out with your grandchildren already.

---

1 week

You are out $10 for a pregnancy test kit and maybe even more money if you bought any clothes recently with waistbands or zippers. The fetus is the size of flea dirt.

---

8 weeks (Two months in non-obstetrical world)

Your friends are already bored with your pregnancy and you are starting to feel permanently bloated. Cocoa Puffs commercials make you cry. The fetus is the size of a cigarette butt.

---

12 weeks (Three months in world with plentiful caffeine)

Your husband says that your choice of Elwood and Winifred as names is hostile. You make plans to enter "Elvis Presley" in the space for father's name on the birth certificate. If you were a ferret you would have given birth by now. The fetus is the size of plastic dog doo-doo.

20 weeks (Five months in regular pantyhose time)

You have passed through the awkward phase of prepartum fat and into pleasingly plump pregnancy. Your husband buys stock in Häagen-Dazs. You tell people who aren't your close friends about your pregnancy. They all know anyway, since all your close friends are no-good rat finks. The fetus is the size of a Barbie doll but not as well developed.

28 weeks (The Third Trimester, or Stretchmark Marathon)

If you were an elephant you would be only halfway to maternity. An average of 3.5 little old ladies per day are rubbing your stomach. Left in an examination room for more than fifteen minutes, you will break off the ceiling tiles and eat them. Don't be surprised if you fall asleep while dialing the telephone or in the middle of performing brain surgery. You have already developed enough milk glands to service the dairy department of a convenience store. The fetus is the size of three gouda cheese balls.

38 weeks (Almost ten months—hey! what happened to the math here?)

Somebody should have told you to prepare for this by walking around with a bowling ball between your legs. The fetus is excreting brain sedatives into your system and has memorized the plots of all the sitcoms you've been watching. Your belly button now has its own name and is making late night calls to your old boyfriends. The fetus still weighs less than your left buttock but has plans to show up when most inconvenient during the next six weeks.

wombs r us

I marvel at a truly enlightened, modern man. He attempts to do what no one (except maybe Cheng and Eng, the famous Siamese Twins) has ever done. He attempts to share another person's internal organ.

"We are pregnant," says the proud father-to-be. To this, I say, "Who's *we*, Testosterone Breath?"

I made it very clear to the Sperm Donor from the beginning that I would hold no truck with that kind of talk.

Not that I am totally unreasonable. If he had demonstrated any interest in sharing my uterus up to this point, I would have gladly let him claim it during its most fruitful months. But did he ever once say, "We are having cramps," or, "We have PMS"? Did he ever say, "We are having a pelvic exam to find out if we have fibroid tumors"?

Not that I recall.

So he's just one of those fair-weather organ users, and I don't need that.

I am pregnant—that's that. Although if this "we" stuff meant I could job out the weight gain and hemorrhoids, I might reconsider.

Newly with child and worried that you won't be able to handle this period of turbulent hormonal change? Just think back to another time in your life, ten to twenty years ago, when you weathered a similar crisis. Pregnancy is much like adolescence, except it's more tiring and *you don't get to leave home when it's over.*

Adolescence vs. Pregnancy: A checklist

Adolescence	*Pregnancy*
Training Bra fitting	Maternity Bra fitting
Worry about losing your virginity	Worry about losing your belly button
Worry excessively about tits	Worry excessively about leaky tits
Strange men yell at you because of developing figure	Strange men yell at you about burgeoning figure
Stay up all hours eating junk food	Wake up at all hours to eat junk food
Not allowed to drink or smoke	Not allowed to drink or smoke
Get to wear first pantyhose	Get to wear first support hose
Experiment with sex	Experiment with new sexual positions

We're pregnant, but only one of us is too sick to get out of bed.

clothing concerns

I've always avoided sports activities requiring the purchase of a specialized wardrobe.

What a surprise to discover that pregnancy is a sort of passive exercise in which your muscles expand beyond what ordinary elastic waistbands can handle. With the very foundation of your garments being threatened by the encroaching parasite, you're left two choices: hiding, or hightailing it down to the Cutesy Name store to buy some duds.

Lady Madonna, Great Expectations, Now Showing—what kind of estrogen high were these shopowners riding when they named these places? They should receive a life sentence of perpetual pregnancy, confined standing up in rolling bus cells and forced to wear T-shirts with arrows pointing downward that say "Baby."

These shops are sex boutiques—everyone in them has had sex and now needs special clothing because of it. I was nervous the first time I entered one, until I saw the other customer in there. This girl gave off tortured vibes that nearly made me forget my own severe caffeine deficiency.

There she was, a high-powered career woman in her late thirties, standing neurotically before the mirror in a blue pinstriped pregnancy suit that made her look like Sydney Greenstreet on hormone therapy.

"I don't know—do you think it makes me look fat?" asked this pathetic sperm victim.

The saleswoman and I exchanged meaningful glances—by meaningful, I mean that we would have burst out laughing if we hadn't been afraid that she was just unstable enough to be carrying a hand grenade in her briefcase.

And so I quickly got in step with the great gestational fashion conspiracy and helped the saleslady get her commission. No, I insisted. How could she even think she looked fat? The pinstriped tent effect actually emphasized all of her good features so much that no one would notice the extra thirty pounds she was already carrying.

Maternity outfits tend to perform this fashion wizardry, you see, by providing unique touches to detract from your belly. These include hefty shoulder pads (I needed ones that were a foot high during my final months) or snug little tight/tunic equations that make you look like Tweedle Dee carrying a purse.

By the time the saleslady and I finished our patter, this fledgling prego-person was feeling pretty good about herself. But little did she know that the trauma would return. Making her purchase, she realized that she would have to carry it back to the office in a "Stork Raving Mad" bag.

"Don't you have a plain bag?" she said. "I can't be seen with this bag."

There ensued quite a tussle, which culminated in the customer frantically searching around in the garbage can and finding a McDonald's bag into which she stuffed her $200 worth of maternity clothing before fleeing.

The saleslady shook her head. "That one! You wouldn't believe it. She was cruising this place for weeks. First she was looking in the window. Then she came in, but she kept saying she was looking for her sister, not for herself. Now, what can I do for you, honey?"

"Um . . . I'm kind of looking for a pair of maternity jeans for my cousin . . ."

the maternity police

As soon as you are noticeably pregnant, you meet the undercover investigators and ruthless enforcers working for The Maternity Police.

These people cruise the streets, shopping malls, corridors of commerce, and even your own home looking for violations.

Maternity law enforcement is a fascinating area, since the laws have never been officially recorded. Instead, they are handed down from little old ladies to hairdressers and magazine reporters for casual dissemination to the public.

I'd like to give you a complete list of pregnancy-related criminal behavior, but the best I can do is offer the transcripts of what the arresting officers said at my own trials in Maternity court.

No vigorous dancing after the sixth month.

Q: What was the suspect doing when apprehended?
A: She was doing the frug at a law firm party.
Q: What did you say as you approached her?
A: I think I said, "Do you think you should shake up your baby that way?"
Q: And what did she say?
A: "Why not?" So I told her a bunch of really good scary stories about late miscarriages.
(Note: In most cases, the sentence for the violation is carried out on the spot and usually involves cruel and unusual punishment, like listening to stories such as the enforcer describes.)

No smoking.

Q: Where did you first observe the suspect?

A: She was attempting to buy cigarettes at a convenience store counter.

Q: And what did she say as you tried to take her into custody?

A: She insisted that she was buying them for a friend of hers who had trouble getting in and out of the car. Ha!

Q: So you didn't believe that?

A: Not for a second. She started yelling when I tried to tell her that she shouldn't be smoking in her delicate condition. I told her she didn't care much about her baby. Then she grabbed the pack of deathsticks and bolted to her car. I must say, she had pretty good wind for a two-hundred-pound pregnant gal who smokes. I watched her get into the car, and it's true that she handed the cigarettes to her friend, who immediately lit one up. But it could have just been a cover. At any rate, I'm glad I finally caught up to her, even if she just faces charges of passive smoking.

No drinking alcohol.

Q: Could you tell us about the circumstances of the arrest?

A: I saw the suspect apprehended sipping a "tasting" size of Chardonnay with dinner at local restaurant. I marched up to her table and said, "Every time you take a drink, so does your baby."

Q: And what did she say?

A: "Good—that means I'm never drinking alone."

Q: Sounds like a nervy girl.

A: Yes, she was feisty. I then went through the major symptoms of fetal alcohol syndrome.

Q: Did she react?

A: She said she didn't think two ounces of wine every week or so could add up to major brain development problems, and that all her mother's friends were busy drinking double martinis while they were pregnant. She asked me if I thought all the babies of foreign countries like France or Italy had brain problems because their mothers drank wine with dinner while they were pregnant.

Q: Do they?

A: Well, you gotta admit that they talk funny, and the men wear sissy shoes.

No drinking tap water.

Q: Where was the arrest made?

A: I cornered her at her own kitchen sink, drinking unfiltered water. "Hey," I said, "do you know what's in that?"

Q: Any reaction?

A: She just looked at me and said, "Yeah—water."

Q: Did you try to enlighten her?

A: Sure, I told her she should have her water supply tested. I told her that when I was pregnant, I had my water, garden soil, air, clothing, and husband tested for carcinogens.

No spraying a bug dead.

Q: Tell us about the case.

A: I overheard her telling everybody at a cocktail party about wearing insect repellent on a hike. She even said she still had her house exterminated once a month.

Q: What did you do?

A: First, I fainted. Then I went out and bought her that book, *How to Respect Insects When You're Expecting*.

No cleaning the Kitty Litter.

Q: How did you first become aware of the violation?

A: I was talking with her over the back fence, and she said something about having to go in to clean the cat's litter box.

Q: What did she say when you told her it was against the law?

A: I've never seen someone so happy to be nailed on one of our regulations. "Now let me get this straight," she said. "My husband has to clean the cat's litter the *entire time* I'm pregnant?" She seemed to enjoy the arrest.

Acceptable Substitutes for Forbidden Items During Pregnancy

1 or 2 glasses of wine	1 or 2 hours of whining
3 cups of coffee	3 chocolate milkshakes
sushi	six shrimp cocktails
aspirin, Tylenol, and other analgesics	extravagant gifts of jewels and cosmetics
hot tubs	hot fudge sundaes

---

do you speak the mother tongue? a vocabulary test

The last time I faced a major vocabulary challenge was the SATs in high school. But as soon as sperm scrambled egg, I was surrounded by amateurs and professionals speaking a language I had never before heard. I offer them here to test your pregnancy vocabulary, or to lessen your learning curve (it might be the only curve you can lessen if you are currently or recently pregnant).

Define the following terms:

1. Braxton Hicks
   A. Pro-Life Senator from Louisiana
   B. National chain of maternity-related legal services.
   C. Creepy little cramps that wake you up but don't mean a thing.

2. Chorionic Villi Sampling (CVS)
   A. Model townhouse development
   B. Antibiotic-of-the-Month Club
   C. Early pregnancy procedure which determines possible abnormalities, sex, and future college choice of fetus.

3. Apgar Test
   A. Standardized determinant of tolerance for Grade B horror movies.
   B. A screening process for algae in toddler wading pools.
   C. Test performed on baby immediately after birth to determine reflexes, respiratory readiness, and amount of obstetrician's bill.

4. Onesie
   A. One-size-fits-all maternity exercise leotard.
   B. A support group for parents of only children.
   C. Over-sized T-shirt that snaps under baby's crotch to give her a svelte no-panty-line look.

5. Colostrum
   A. Ancient stadium built for fertility rituals, recently excavated near Rome.
   B. New bran product designed to reduce cholesterol.
   C. Strange pre-milk fluid that protects your newborn from disease, allergies, and bad first marriages.

6. RH Factor
   A. A formula which takes the hours of postpartum REM (R) sleep, multiplies it against the hours of paid help (H) you have, and predicts the number of weeks until complete mental collapse.
   B. An inability to master simple song lyrics, noticed in kids whose parents refuse to allow children's folksong tapes into their homes (Raffi-Holdout Factor).
   C. Difficulties which occur when one parent has a positive blood type and the other a negative type or attitude.

7. Breech position
   A. A clause in the release forms you sign before going into the delivery room.
   B. Sexual technique for the last two weeks of pregnancy.
   C. Feet-first position of baby that indicates you will be giving birth to either a hiker or a shoe-addicted disciple of Imelda Marcos.

8. VBAC
   A. Adults who do not excel at children's games (Very Bad at Candyland).
   B. Slang term for foxy pregnant women (Very Big and Cute)
   C. Vaginal Birth After Caesarean, also known as the worst of both worlds—pelvic pain, and scarring, too!

9. Meconium
   A. Latin term for any touching lullaby sung to baby between three and four in the morning.
   B. New antiseptic solution for boo-boos.
   C. An especially disgusting pre-poop substance that exudes from newborns.

10. Pitocin
    A. Vitamin which improves your child's chances of someday spitting out watermelon pits.
    B. New gymboree-like program in which newborns swim in pits of Jell-O.
    C. Synthesized hormone injected into a woman's bloodstream to speed labor and sharpen contractions and her desire to murder anyone in the vicinity.

Scoring: Everything in the C-section is correct. One to three incorrect answers indicate Anti-Mom tendencies; more than three indicates either an extreme estrogen deficiency or mental illness.

in the swim

Hester Prynne wore the Scarlet A. In this liberal era, our society has devised a more potent punishment for sex. It is called the maternity swimsuit.

Mine made me cry the first time I tried it on. Being a masochist, I figured it was the one for me. Actually, I had tried on a few that could be construed as moderately "cute," but then the saleslady barged into my dressing room to attach the hideous pregnancy pillow to my stomach (I was only four months along then and had no idea of the potential elasticity of the female form). "Hon," she said, "this is never gonna do. You see—you're tall. You're gonna need more stretch in the thing."

So she brought out the real tearjerker, kept on reserve for the hugest of the hormonally impaired. The thing was the size of a VW beetle, and black with big white polka dots all over it. This swimsuit captured that oh-so-special look at the top of any woman's fashion agenda: Bozo swallows a watermelon.

I wore it, of course. I was happy for it, in the end. The thing allowed me to float in water and forget that I weighed over 200 pounds. During the last week of my pregnancy, I heard a guy gasp as I pulled myself up out of the pool. I couldn't tell if it was the sheer spectacle of the suit or his understandable worry that I might have left amniotic fluid in his lane.

a.d. 2093

—ARCHAEOLOGISTS DISCOVER HOMESTEAD
OF LAST ELDERLY PRIMIGRAVIDA—
NATURAL PREGNANCY MUSEUM TO OPEN

Almost nine months ago, construction workers breaking ground for the new Hovercraft station in Trumpstate near Clintonville came upon an amazing find: the actual home of one of the so-called "elderly primigravidas" of the waning days of the twentieth century.

The term "elderly primigravida" was used by the medical profession to describe women who postponed having their first child until after age thirty, when their careers were firmly established. This strategy was necessary before the days of pregnancy growth tank centers and nationalized toddler farms. The home, already designated a National Historic site, is about to open its doors to the public.

"This is a very important find," says Madonna Storkley, the director of the new Natural Pregnancy Museum. "Until now, we have had to rely on oral histories and old *I Love Lucy* episodes to give us an impression of what it was like to be over thirty and naturally pregnant. But, somehow, miraculously, this home was preserved, and we can see how a person under the influence of heavy hormones actually lived."

Storkley, who is twenty-five and mother of six-year-old sextuplets hatched at the Little Tadpoles Spawning Center, gave a preview tour of the site. Some of the exhibit highlights:

Strange, Impressionistic Portraits of Fetuses   Entering by the back door, explorers found several of these blurry pictures attached to the refrigerator by Mickey Mouse–shaped magnets. Historians believe they were taken by the father with some sort of miniature camera set at the wrong speed. These are now displayed in an interactive format—visitors push buttons to guess which body part is which.

Large White Harness with Wire Underpinnings   Was this an implement of torture or just an undergarment of some kind? Historians disagree about whether this uncomfortable harness, with a label reading "Maternity Bra," was worn as a constant reminder of error, like a hair shirt, or if it really served some useful purpose. Structural experts marvel at the garment's construction, believing it to be the work of a demented aeronautical engineer. In a special note to this exhibit, one scholar theorizes that pregnant women might have naturally craved a preview of the lingerie selections that would be available to them as seventy-year-olds.

Dish Filled with Rings   The bedroom was a treasure trove of information because of the vast pregnancy-related library found stacked at the side of the bed. Before museum curators consulted one of the tomes, *How to Gain Sixty Pounds in Nine Easy Months*, they believed that pregnant women left jewelry around in piles as tributes to the fertility gods. Now we know that physiological changes such as swelled digits and bellies replaced jewelry as status symbols during the pregnancy period.

Giant Two-Sided Pillow That Looks Like a Lima Bean   Did the husband and wife somehow share this device? Did they use it as a lovemaking aid? Or did the pregnant woman perform a nightly ritual of making herself into a fat sausage sandwich? Scholars are still debating.

Breathing Exercise Tapes   (Audio Exhibit) Found in primitive tape machine. The in-body growth of the fetus apparently made women forget how to breathe. Visitors can listen as a patient narrator tutors women in the art of pregnant respiration, an obviously labored event which required much huffing and puffing.

preparing for the event

Can you really respect any Lamaze class that schedules itself opposite Monday Night Football? These people are supposed to have thought of everything to make your completely natural childbirth a prepared, organized, and fulfilling experience. Yet how could my husband pay attention when he was listening to the game on a Walkman? (Later, during the birth, he grabbed our daughter by the head and passed her under his legs to the midwife.)

Sports competition wasn't the only annoying thing about our class. There we were, sitting around with five other couples with whom we had nothing in common except that the women were all as blimpy and hormonally whacked-out as I was. The sessions resembled those endless sex education lectures in gym class, only they were more embarrassing because they were coed. I loved the fascinating diagrams about how your stomach and intestines end up somewhere near your eyeballs as your pregnancy expands, but I balked when it came to discussing my constipation with a group of total strangers.

Midway through each class, interaction descended to the kindergarten level. The instructor asked cutely if all the girls had to go to the potty, which, of course, we did, since our bladders were now pushed up under our left armpits and had become the size of Tic-Tacs. Then we enjoyed snacky time, with cookies, fruit juice, and milk.

After the break the toys came out, including the plastic pelvis, the plastic uterus, and the fake baby. We'd all get turns playing with them, seeing how they fit together and popped out. Just like in grade school, the girls flocked around the dolly, while the boys fought over the baby-factory machinery parts.

At the end of each session, we climbed onto the floor to practice our Lamaze breathing.

"Okay, men," said our cheery labor instructor (who looked exactly like my high school gym teacher, except that she wasn't wearing a kilt). "Now I want you to pinch your wife's thigh to simulate the pain of a labor contraction. Women, you go into your early-stage breathing for the length of the pinch."

It worked great the first time. Al pinched me, and I decked him. He pinched me again, and I started to cry.

Was this what labor would be like?

It turns out it was.

labor simplified

Labor instructors and birthing books will confuse you by referring in great detail to different methods of relaxation, but it all boils down to three approaches. Read these handy summaries and you can skip childbirth preparation altogether.

The Surfer Girl Strategy   Labor contractions, say the birth manuals, are much like ocean waves, coming in rhythmic patterns. A gal who can ride those waves of pain with panache will have an easier time of it. Of course, she might end up naming the kid Moondoggie afterwards. Hang ten (hours)!

The L.L. Bean Model Approach   Some manuals encourage you to visualize your child's head coming through your cervix in much the same way that your own head pops through the opening of a turtleneck sweater. Only two problems: Putting on a sweater rarely takes thirty-six hours, and when the turtleneck is made out of your own flesh, it just doesn't stretch as well as Lycra. (Our childbirth instructor pushed a baby doll through a turtleneck opening over and over again—it's been four years now, and just the sight of some preppie model in a cotton turtleneck makes me start to sweat.)

The Navel-Gazing Sixties Be-In Having a baby is like giving birth to yourself, say the groovy birth gurus, and the pain can help you focus on the spiritual nature of the event. One book recommends choosing a Birth Mantra to chant over and over again. I didn't realize until I went into labor that I had subconsciously chosen my mantra: "Get This Baby Out of Me." Optional be-in labor marathon accessories include burning incense and candles, Jacuzzis, and new age Muzak tapes.

honing your labor pain vocabulary

When you're pregnant, you're like a magnet for the Ancient Mariners of pelvic pain. These are the sadistic ladies who stop you on the street and in line at the supermarkets to tell their labor horror stories.

"Ninety-six hours! The doctor had just told my husband to get his shotgun out and put me out of my misery when our son's head appeared."

"Five years! I couldn't sit down for five years after I gave birth. Since I had four kids, that means my dinette chair is still like new."

The pains of labor are world famous, and why shouldn't they be? Even Madonna can't muster that much free publicity.

Well, I'm here to offer a minority opinion. Labor is not as bad as it's cracked up to be. Sure, it hurts like hell. But then it's over. What you should really worry about are the next eighteen years—they're painful in a much slower way, like peeling a huge adhesive bandage off your brain, cell by cell.

That said, you must not neglect having a labor horror story to tell friends, relatives, and pregnant women you bump into at cocktail parties for the rest of your life. It is also a good idea to hone such a story for telling to your kid when he is acting up.

So here's a crib sheet of words and phrases for making yours the scariest labor story yet—it will help you enormously in the game of Dueling Dilation, which is played at baby showers, hairstylists, and health clubs across the nation. The cardinal rule of the game: No matter how bad someone else's labor was, yours was worse.

Adjectives and phrases for the pain:

piercing, excruciating, mind-numbing
one billion times worse than cramps
like crawling through broken glass
like being kicked in the stomach by an elephant wearing cleats
like a nest of vicious, pressing beetles
like a demonic bowling ball rolling through internal space
like passing a pumpkin
like an umbrella opening up inside my stomach . . .

Adjectives and phrases to describe the medical staff attending you:

nastier than Carrie's gym teacher
resembled Nurse Ratched from *One Flew Over the Cuckoo's Nest*
Have you seen Jeremy Irons in *Dead Ringers*?

Length of Time Reference

longer than two showings of the complete *I, Claudius*
like a Jerry Lewis Telethon
longer than a PBS fund drive
I finally understood how the Iranian Hostages felt

HANDY TIPS

Things to Take Along to Your Birthing Experience

Paper Bag for putting over your head as you begin to look really bad;
Tapes, candles, tennis balls, and other toys for your husband to fiddle with while you writhe in pain;
Money to bribe the nurses for drugs;
A spare, fresh husband for when the first one gives out during long labor;
Urine specimen so that you can convince the nurses that you've "eliminated" after you've given birth.

Nesting Instinct Substitutes

Busy, busy, busy—that's what you'll want to be when that old nesting instinct wells up inside your tuberous body. To avoid doing something really stupid like tearing down your house, why not try one of the following time-consuming but useless hobbies?

Build shoebox dioramas of hospital delivery rooms.
Sculpt fertility goddess figurines out of Play-Doh.
Make an infant car seat out of popsicle sticks.
Dissect a Cabbage Patch Doll.
Make paper clip stirrups for pregnant gerbils.
Plant Mr. Potato Head.
Make necklaces from leftover birth control pills.
Convert sock hangers into a baby mobile.

what to say to people at your baby shower

Baby showers are stressful for the ill-prepared. They resemble an anthropological expedition—opening each gift, you are forced to figure out its meaning and significance in the child-rearing culture, often with very little context.

Don't betray your ignorance or risk having your baby whisked away from you immediately after birth. Use this handy chart to correctly identify gifts and thank people graciously and accurately.

If it looks like . . .	It probably is . . .
An inflatable condom	A faucet protector to keep baby from bumping her head at bathtime
A winestopper with a handle	A pacifier
A cappuccino machine	An electric breast pump
Dishcloths with a place to put your hand	Hooded baby towels
A sex-aid nightgown that allows your husband to fondle your breasts	A nursing nightgown

Gifts I Wish I Had Received at My Baby Shower

Year's supply of Valium
Full-time nanny
Gift certificate for tummy tuck and liposuction
Extra husband to help with night feedings

ask anti-mom

Dear Anti-Mom,

How can I remain desirable to my husband now that I am eight months pregnant?

Tubby in Toledo

Dear Tubby,

Feeling sexy in late pregnancy is simply a matter of adjusting your fantasies. By planning ahead, you can surprise your husband with fun scenarios and costume changes:

Sexy Sumo Wrestling: He comes through the door to see that you have replaced your living room furniture with raked sand and small wooden platforms. Before he can get his bearings, you leap from behind a very large Bonsai, your hair slicked back in a ponytail and wearing nothing but an attractive white thong. A few grunts, and you're saying "Sayonara" to the blues.

The Honeymooners: Nostalgia and sex are a potent combination when you get a bus driver's uniform and play the role of Ralph Kramden in those third trimester lovemaking sessions. And away we go . . .

Fertility Goddess: You'll look ravishing swathed only in rose petals, seated in front of heaps of fatty foods, and demanding obeisance. Most men adore making love to the Source of All Life on Our Planet.

Dear Anti-Mom,

My spouse and I are arguing about name choices. What are your recommendations?

Nameless in Nevada

Dear Nameless,

Tops on my list are Visa, for a girl, and MasterCard for a boy. Why? Because I believe in naming kids after someone you're indebted to.

are those violins i'm hearing?

If you had the choice of spending the evening with
  A. A world-famous violinist, or
  B. A screaming woman with ooze coming down her legs, which would you choose?
  If you answered "A," then you would have been sympathetic to the sperm donor on the evening of our Blessed Event.
  After consultations with little old ladies and male veterans of child-birthing, he had decided that our first kid would be at least two weeks late. So he went out and got tickets to see violinist Pinchas Zuckerman on the night of my due date.
  As the date approached and I looked more and more like I was going to explode any minute, Alan started worrying that his night out on the town was in jeopardy. He began a campaign to convince me that culture *could* triumph over biology. If only I would hold out, he promised, he'd buy me a glass of champagne after the concert. He'd change

the baby's diapers for the first three months. He'd even take the kid to Disney World some day.

I was willing, but the fetus wasn't. We were taking a walk on the morning of the concert when—whoosh! a sudden puddle announced that Kelly would soon be *ex utero*.

Dad still wasn't ready to give up. He shook his fist at my belly: "Why couldn't you wait—one more lousy day. Geez!"

And then he tried to convince me that I could still go. Why, I wasn't in labor yet, was I? No, I conceded, as I went upstairs to change my clothes. No, I just had a lot of gooshy stuff oozing down my leg and would probably be giving birth to my first child pretty darn soon. I'd be delighted to get all dressed up and sit still for three hours at a classical music concert. Perhaps the first violinist could deliver the baby. Maybe it would be a boy and we could call him Pinchas.

I called my best friend, who couldn't believe that I was even considering going to the concert with this madman. She thought that my husband's suggestion should make me think twice about even putting his name down on the birth certificate. "You're having a *baby*," she said. "What's one goddamn concert?"

I guess a guy thinks differently. To my husband, this concert represented his one last fling, his swan song of childlessness. The possibility that my afterbirth might splatter an old lady's mink coat didn't occur to him at all.

My husband has a way of talking me into ridiculous situations. We once drove over the Alps in a snowstorm because he thought it would be fun. Could this be any worse than that experience?

I called my nurse midwife. If active labor hadn't started, she said, I *could* attend the concert. Wondering if I should confess this news to my future labor coach, I hung up the phone. As the receiver touched down, I felt the first contraction.

A double feature of Cary Grant movies on the tube got me through the next few hours as my husband sulked and my cervix began opening. Dazed and in a bit of pain, I found myself fantasizing that I was having Cary Grant's baby. Of course, Cary probably would have wanted to go to the Monte Carlo casino while I was having his baby.

But there on the t.v., Cary looked a lot better as a potential labor companion than my husband, who was pacing back and forth, wondering when he should call the symphony box office to turn in our tickets and get a charitable deduction. He was still praying fervently for a diagnosis of false labor.

"Don't mind me," I said one time during a commercial and between contractions. "Just go—enjoy yourself at the concert. I'll take a cab. I'm sure our baby will understand that you had a date. We can put the concert program in the baby book."

He finally gave in when the contractions were five minutes apart and I was about to head out the door. Of course, he took a couple of minutes to let the guy at the box office know that he was only giving up the tickets under duress (he had the sound effects of my moaning as background to prove it). But I have to say, he was very gracious after we got into the car. He only mentioned the concert two or three times.

three childbirth techniques i'd like to see become popular

Leary Method: As soon as you go into labor, you receive a dose of LSD that will last at least eighteen years. Would make motherhood even more of a trip than it already is.

Hotel Birthing: Couples check into that special "get-away" birthing suite. Jacuzzi, room service, bellhop obstetricians—what more could a girl want?

Fetal Bungie-Jumping: Why make birth a soothing experience, when we well know that mostly stress and risk-taking lie ahead for our offspring? In this method, mom would stand on a raised platform with a big hole cut out of it, and baby would make a daring plunge into the world, bouncing by the cord and arriving to a standing ovation. A real rush!

the anti-mom film festival

Skip Jane Fonda's pregnancy exercise tapes. You need other types of videos, ones that will really show you what it is like to give birth or interact with children. So sit back, prop up your swollen tootsies, and *enjoy*!

Rating System:

☹☹☹☹ Four Contractions: Better than Pitocin

☹☹☹ Three Contractions: More Exciting Than a Braxton-Hicks

☹☹ Two Contractions: Beats a Pelvic Exam

☹ One Contraction: As Much Fun as Peeing in a Cup

Rosemary's Baby (1968)☹☹☹☹. The grandmammy of all pregnancy angst films, starring Mia Farrow (queen of relationship angst) and John Cassavetes. The devil made her do it—he made her have his baby, and now there's hell to pay. A completely realistic film except for that nice apartment young struggling actor Cassavetes seems able to rent in Manhattan.

The Seventh Sign (1988) ☹☹☹. A pregnant pre-pinup Demi Moore is haunted (no, not by Patrick Swayze) by either an emissary of the devil or an angel who wants her to know that she is carrying the antichrist or the true messiah. She manages to keep her makeup intact during labor and looks good even on her deathbed.

The Fly (remake, 1986) ☹☹☹☹ (for fake Fly-birth scene only). Dramatically portrays what it's like to give birth to a giant insect (although it could be worse, since the fly baby will surely look a little bit like Jeff Goldblum). One of the best pregnancy paranoia sequences ever filmed. But the question is never answered: Should Geena Davis get in a large supply of flypaper instead of a playpen?

The Miracle of Morgan's Creek (1944) ☹☹. A drunken Betty Hutton's ovaries release too many eggs on just the right night. Madcap farcical tone cannot totally mask the horror of the final sextuplet birth sequence.

The Bad Seed (1956) ☹☹. Flash forward to six-year-old murderess Patty McCormack, who is enough to scare any new mom silly. Blonde, adorable, and willing to kill a wimpy boy just for a spelling medal.

The Omen (1976) ☹. Adoption—who knows who you'll get—a normal kid or THE DEVIL'S SON !!!! A sobering look at early childhood education.

Alien (- - -) ☹☹☹. (For alien popping out of stomach scene). Every woman's nightmare of caesarean section gone awry.

Demon Seed (1977) ☹☹. The movie that asks the question: Would a computer make a better Lamaze coach than a real guy? Julie Christie mates with the computer that runs her house. A sequel never released shows her breastfeeding a laptop.

And now, a preview of coming distractions . . .

Some Tips for Prepared Child*rearing*

Everyone talks about prepared *childbirth*, but what about the next phase? Here are some steps you can take to get yourself ready for the days ahead.

Buy a box of Adult Size diapers and practice putting them on your husband.

Go through your closet and smear cream cheese on all your favorite blouses.

During the day: Put a timer on for 4 minutes; when it goes off, cease whatever you are doing—reading, cooking, making love, watching television, doing laundry—and run frantically to another room.

At night: Set your alarm clock for every two hours. When it rings, make your husband get up to feed and burp the cat.

PART II

bootie camp

The thing has emerged, denial has set in, and you fight
for your physical and emotional turf . . .

brainwashing secrets of the newborn

Does the maternal instinct exist or is it a figment of the imagination? Could it be that the imagination gets figged by factors totally out of your control—that you're duped into thinking you're hopelessly attached to a lump of flesh that weighs less than a Butterball turkey?

Looking back, I can see the brainwashing taking place in several steps, both *in* and *ex utero*.

For nine months, you have been tortured with nausea and fatigue. You've been kicked constantly from within. You've been denied many of your favorite foods, drugs, and beverages, and your regular clothes have been taken away from you.

And then the baby exits, and, like all good hostages, you learn to love your captor.

Soon you're deep into the spirit-breaking atmosphere of bootie camp. You can't get more than two hours' of sleep at a stretch. You're afraid to go to the bathroom because the baby might start crying or because you might see yourself in the mirror. You are presented with an endless series of seemingly simple tasks that are actually fairly impossible, like holding and bathing a fatty blob with no neck muscles.

The Curse of the Mommy has come shrieking out of the womb. Overnight, you have gone from being a kind of cute pregnant person to an obese, milk-producing zombie. So what? You must still pretend that YOUR LIFE HAS NOT CHANGED A BIT.

Believe me, denial is the only way to go. And, with that in mind, I recommend taking those first postpartum weeks to formulate a manifesto that will steady your resolve during the next few years of motherhood.

The Anti-Mom Manifesto

- I will continue to wear dry-clean-only garments.
- I will not lose my gag reflex no matter how many disgusting bodily secretions I see.
- I will never say "cootchy-coo."
- I will try my best never to spit on my baby to clean her.
- I will not worry about my baby's excrement output, nor will I talk about it.
- I will never actually eat Cheerios.
- I will never learn to use a rectal thermometer
- I will continue to believe that bonding is for teeth.

is there life after birth?

No wonder most women get a little depressed after giving birth.

You've met this enormous biological deadline. You've pulled an all-nighter to pop that baby out, and now you want to think the whole thing is over. But it's not over by any stretch of the imagination, even though the fat lady screamed. You've just hatched the most time-consuming hobby ever conceived.

Just where does all that time go when the baby is brand new? That's what your husband will ask when he gets home from work and you are still wearing your bathrobe. Here is a reckoning.

Diapering

Tougher than it looks. I was putting Kelly's disposable diaper on backwards for the first week until my sister-in-law came to visit and corrected my mistake. I had just assumed that the disgusting cartoon character band should go in the back. How was I to know that it was meant to enhance the thing? Thank God I didn't have to learn to use safety pins, like my mother, who when I was a baby took me to a pediatrician visit with my diaper fastened to my flesh.
(Average time spent per day: 2 hours)

Burping

A confession: I never actually burped Kelly, but I spent a lot of time trying. After a while she seemed like a human Ouija board. I would put her on my lap and move my hand around her back until I convinced myself that the burp had communicated from beyond, even though I never really heard it. My nightmare is that when she's nineteen,

sitting in some college class, one giant burp will finally escape and blow down the building.
(Time spent per day: 1 hour)

Swaddling

I never knew anyone did this outside of biblical circles. Wrapping a little square of flannel around a kicking baby is even harder than wrapping Christmas presents, something I don't do very well. (Is that why they call them receiving blankets?)
(Time spent per day: 2 hours)

Walking around with the baby

It took a while to figure out the geometry. Maybe most new moms don't admit it, but I had a hard time judging where Kelly's head was as I turned the corners or went upstairs. Infants' heads should come with protective Styrofoam packaging. Until I got the knack of walking around encumbered, the poor kid was constantly in danger of becoming The Thing That Went Bump in the Night.
(Time spent per day and night: 3 hours)

Arguing and crying

Wildly fluctuating hormonal levels made this seem like the perfect time to confront my mother about a favorite pair of socks that she shrank by mistake when I was in the third grade. I also remember trying to clear the air by calling my husband at the office to confront him about something he did on our second date.
(Time spent per day: 2 hours)

Reading your stretch marks

Better than palm reading, and more constructive than navel-gazing (especially since your navel is still all screwed up).
(Time spent per day: 1 hour)

Making new best friends

Meet Oprah, Phil, and Geraldo. They care about you, and they enjoy introducing you to people whose newborns weren't even hatched on this planet.
(Time spent per day: 3 hours)

Your Newborn Baby: Some Comparisons

If you're like any other parent, you're anxious to know how your baby stacks up as a brand-new human being. You have probably read the early chapters of your baby-rearing books over and over, trying to reconcile the exciting portrait of the newborn presented there with the potato-like object now residing in your house.

Here's a better comparative guide to the unique characteristics of the newborn.

NEWBORN BABY .... ROCK
Baby is softer; rock is quieter. Personalities are about the same.

NEWBORN BABY .... CAT
Baby cannot jump up on counter; cat does not require diapers or nose syringe. Cat is more intelligent and interactive.

NEWBORN BABY .... NUCLEAR BOMB
Baby changes face of human life as you know it; bomb does same thing, but does not make a lot of laundry afterwards.

Boiling and washing things

Nipples, T-shirts, bottles, breast cups, blankets—all of this stuff has to be sanitized on a tight rotating schedule. The water company called

me during those first few weeks just to see if we had installed an Olympic-size swimming pool.
(Time spent per day: 4 hours)

Total Time: 18 hours, which leaves another whole six for rest and relaxation.

crazy glue

There are some things you just don't know until after you give birth. For example, I discovered that I married a bonding freak.

Don't you think this bonding stuff has been carried a bit too far? For mothers, whether or not bonding exists is a moot point—you're pretty much automatically bonded to anyone you spend twenty-four hours a day around, especially if that little person's mouth is attached to one of your nipples about seventy-five percent of the time.

But it's a guy-thing to worry about bonding. Men bond with their friends by drinking a lot of beer, and they expect to do it with their infants, only they're somewhat at a loss as to what to do when their potential bonding partner only drinks breast milk. Someone even tried to ease this problem by inventing a "nursing bra" for men, a fabric sling that enables them to attach bottles to their chests and dupe babies into thinking that they're getting the real thing. My husband didn't put in an order for one of those because it might have eliminated his excuses for not getting up in the middle of the night. But Al *was* overly concerned from the first that Kelly recognize his Daddyness and become affixed to his person. Each evening he would get home from work and strip off his shirt so that the two of them could bond skin to skin in front of the t.v. set.

What was going through Kelly's head? "Now let me get this

straight—the one with the hairy chest doesn't give milk, but they let him hang around watching basketball anyway." She was perfectly amenable to falling asleep on the hairy one, if she wasn't hungry. So there they would sit, night after night, Kelly glued to Al, and Al glued to the television set. Al would only move his arm slightly to switch channels, while Kelly dozed like a hairless cat, limp against his chest.

One night when Kelly was barely two weeks old, Al had an infant-bonding/male-bonding experience with his best friend, who also stripped to the waist for the ritual. They passed Kelly back and forth the way they used to pass a pipe, only more gingerly. "Wow, this is, like, unbelievable," said my husband's friend Bruce, getting high on infant contact.

"Yeah, isn't it?" said my husband dreamily.

I had to leave the room because I suddenly felt my morning sickness returning, but I understand that they were about to build a sweat hut and sing Native American lullabies when Kelly woke up and started crying.

"Here—I think she's hungry," said my husband as he handed over the bawling infant and went out to the kitchen to grab a few beers.

New Age Bonding Rituals for Moms

Don't fall into a bonding rut! Add a little excitement to your infant-mom sessions. Here's what I tried. (I wanted to make sure that my daughter would not feel overly bonded and come back to live with me after her third marriage.)

- Replicate the pattern of your varicose veins on your baby's legs with washable Magic Marker.
- Put the scab from your baby's new belly button in a locket and wear it close to your heart.
- Whisper the personal identification number for your automatic teller card in your baby's ear.

the booby prize: breastfeeding for amateurs

You spend a lot of time in girlhood worrying about when you're going to get tits. Then you waste those next years worrying about whether guys will like the tits you end up with.

And then, in the last few weeks of being held hostage by the fetal intruder, the thought begins to gnaw:

Somebody could *eat* off these things?

It was hard to imagine at first. As much as I looked at diagrams showing how a breast was just like a bottle, I still couldn't believe that mine could sustain human life, any more than I can believe that our backyard can sustain grass. Bottles seemed a pretty good unnatural kind of idea, like AstroTurf. Besides—could somebody as nasty as me possess the milk of human kindness?

But the breastfeeding lobby was after me from the start. They leafletted the house with literature outlining what would happen if I didn't suckle my young:

1. It would develop no immune system and have to live in a bubble on a t.v. movie for the rest of its life.
2. It would be allergic to pollen, combustion engines, and PBS children's programs.
3. It would either be bloated and fat enough to star in the "before" pictures for baby NutriSystem billboards or emaciated enough to appear in a Sally Struthers ad.

People Who Were Probably Breastfed as Babies

Lizzie Borden	Carrie Nation
Attila the Hun	Al Capone
Adolf Hitler	Jack the Ripper
Catharine the Great	Dracula
Benito Mussolini	

Eventually I nippled under and began reading some of the stuff, which appealed to my natural egomania. The whole female power trip began to sweep me away—I mean, we *are* the only sex that can produce a body fluid that's not totally noxious. Then I received a brochure about breastfeeding *consultants*. For a fee, these trained lactation specialists would come to my house and teach me to do what comes naturally. I don't even use consultants for my wardrobe—I mean, how complicated could this nursing stuff be?

Very.

It seemed that the incredibly empowering TOTALLY NATURAL act of breastfeeding took hours of preparation, practice, and shopping. People have written whole books on it, taking up endless pages on the regimen of nipple toughening exercises alone, all of which seemed to involve rough towels and no fun. Reading about these exercises was similar to watching t.v. exercise shows. I didn't actually *do* the exercises, but somehow I thought my nipples might get in shape just by being in proximity to the books.

The decision to nurse my kid also meant the purchase of a complete line of titty-related products, including gross pads that look like old lady dress shields, special bras with trapdoors, small petrie dishes for collecting milk specimens, and hand-held pumping equipment that seemed a dead ringer for the Mark Eden Bust Developer machines featured in the backs of magazines when I was fourteen.

This was obviously going to be a high-maintenance activity. Still, the prospects for fulfillment seemed good. My kid would be given the best possible start at becoming Emperor of the Universe—an allergy-free, disease-resistant, thin-for-life Emperor of the Universe. And the books promised that I would feel perpetually orgasmic from the massive amounts of oxytocin pumping through my body.

Both these goals, it turns out, involved a great deal of deferred gratification. Before my baby could start on her way to becoming a revered demigod, for example, she had to learn to Latch On.

Latching On is sort of similar to NASA space missions in which the spaceship and satellite connect, only the astronauts do not scream while it is happening. The first time Kelly Latched On to my unexercised nipple, I let loose with a yell that set back our bonding process for weeks. Toothless, but ruthless—that's how I began to see the human baby's quest for sustenance. Eventually, I substituted my old Lamaze breathing techniques for the screaming.

Once the nipples have hardened up (and they *do*, becoming a little bit like leather elbow patches misplaced), the pain subsides.

But even cows get the blues, so I decided on some hard and fast ground rules right from the beginning:

1. No bare boobs in public. I was going to try my darnedest not to expose my mammaries to the elements or to prying eyes. This got harder as I became more reluctant to sit for hours in toilet stalls, and as my attempts at discreet public breastfeeding got thwarted by an increasingly active baby who seemed intent on actively massaging the source of her food supply.
2. No high-tech accoutrements. I tried pumping once and decided that there are better uses for suction in my life. If my breasts weren't available, Kelly could sip one of the wonderful formulas provided by the pharmaceutical industry—I was willing to risk the loss of a few I.Q. points.

3. Six months and out. I had no desire to suckle a child who could do a critical review of a Barney the Dinosaur episode or use anatomically correct terms to request a drink.

Probably that last rule is why I never reached the perpetually orgasmic state that some breastfeeding moms are supposed to enjoy. Maybe I just needed more practice.

Bosom Buddy Facts at a Glance

Bottlefeeding vs.	**Breastfeeding**
Many new, attractive models of bottles available.	Human mammary glands do not come with pictures of Mickey Mouse, but temporary tattoos are a possibility.
You always know just how much your baby is drinking.	You always know how much your boobs hurt.
You can feed your baby anywhere (as long as you remember the formula, can opener, bottles, nipples, bottle warmer . . .)	It is very difficult to forget your breasts when you leave the house.
You will be immune to the stares of lecherous men and little old ladies who complain to restaurant maitre d's.	Your baby will only catch 27 colds the first two years instead of 33.

vital stats

Whoever said that size doesn't matter wasn't talking about babies. People are obsessed by infant statistics. Since I have trouble with numbers, it took a while to learn the ropes, but I'll pass some tips along.

It's best to imagine your kid as a baseball rookie who gradually amasses career stats as she grows. Everyone will want to know exactly how much the new rookie weighs, how long she is, and what her big-league growth potential is. Rounding off to the nearest pound is never acceptable. A birth announcement should list your baby's weight and height in kilos and centimeters as well as pounds and inches. Include her percentile rating, too, and maybe an estimate of how many of her it would take to equal the height of the Empire State Building, or how she compares weightwise to other mammals, reptiles, or favorite candies. (I offered the helpful analogy that you would have to eat 9,473 M&Ms to equal Kelly's weight.)

Now, just because you can't round off to the nearest pound on the announcement doesn't mean you shouldn't lie about your child's weight when strangers ask, depending on how you feel that day. After all, you have plenty of practice lying about your own weight. So when a nosy lady came up to me in the mall and said, "My, that's a big baby—how much did she weigh at birth?" I always said fourteen pounds, three ounces, and added that her head was the biggest ever recorded in the tri-state area.

I thought memorizing vital birth stats would be enough, but it doesn't stop there. Everyone wants to know how many ounces of milk your baby is drinking per day. I had no idea, mostly because the ounces were coming from my body. But I always said sixty-eight ounces, without blinking an eye, even when the questioner would point out that it was physically impossible.

Occasionally, these statistical things can ruin your life. My friend Sally wants to sue her pediatrician because the second time she took her baby to be weighed, a nurse read the scale wrong and reported that he had lost two pounds. The doctor, alarmed, ordered Sally to wake the baby up every three hours to feed him, even though he was sleeping through the night. After that, he didn't sleep through the night for another two years, and it turned out that he had "gained" eleven pounds the next time he saw the doctor, who had to admit that there must have been a mistake.

These kinds of stories are scary: That's why I recommend carrying along fishing weights that you can slip into your baby's diaper right as she goes onto the scale. Better to err on the heavy side, and really let your baby enjoy this one time in her life when gaining lots of weight is the cool thing to do.

Infant clothing sizes also indicate a cultural obsession with size. First, the manufacturers give you a head start by labeling all the newborn garments "3 months." So the day your baby comes home she is already precociously mature in her fashion tastes, and by the time she is a month old she's wearing things that say "6–9 months." People ask you what size she is wearing, and you're ridiculously proud to state these inflated sizes. Of course, spending a few bucks to get size-2 labels made for all your own clothing would do just as much for your ego.

Kelly was three months old and wearing clothes supposedly designed for a one-year-old when I finally awoke to the deception. I was starting to get panicky, thinking that I had given birth to a future fifty-foot woman. At this rate of growth, would she be wearing a training bra by the time she was fourteen months old? Could I expect her to start borrowing my sweaters before she could even hold her neck steady? And then the hormones wore off, and I saw clearly that I was a dupe of the baby clothing industry.

After that, when interested bystanders would casually ask Kelly's size, I would go in the opposite direction just to see how they would react. "Oh—we're not even into baby sizes yet. She still fits in my old Barbie doll clothes."

Revised Percentile Bragging Points

New parents love knowing that their kid is in the upper 90s in percentile for height and weight. But what if scrawny, dwarfish genes run in your family, or if you keep losing that little booklet the pediatrician fills in at each visit? Don't worry—it is the high 90s number that people hear, and they seldom listen to the category involved. So you can brag without lying by using some of these . . .

93rd percentile in name length
97th percentile in stuffed animal ownership
100th percentile in helplessness
99th percentile in sheet change frequency
96th percentile in vocal decibels
92nd percentile in birth control effectiveness

horoscopes for newborns

A new day dawns (maybe even pre-dawns), and if you're lucky you get a spare two minutes to sneak a quick look at your newspaper horoscope. All the wonderful predictions about jobs and torrid romances now seem like jokes. Let's face it—of the two of you, your newborn baby is living a more exciting life. Here's a set of horoscopes specifically designed for those under six weeks of age. (There is only one for each sign, because it is good for every day.)

ARIES: You might feel like crying today—indulge yourself!

TAURUS: Is there lots of curdled crap bottled up inside you? Now is the time to let the bad stuff spew forth.

GEMINI: Let somebody push you around today—it will be worth it.

CANCER: Today you feel like you could piss all over the world, but it will only get you the kind of attention you don't want.

LEO: The people around you are trying to rattle your nerves, but just close your eyes and think of floating.

VIRGO: Whine enough, and you might have a swinging time in store for you.

LIBRA: Life sucks for you today and will continue to.

SCORPIO: Take it easy—spend the day lazing around and eating as much as you want.

SAGITTARIUS: You'll be amazed how one little smile from you can excite everyone in the room. Play along, even though you have bad gut feelings.

CAPRICORN: The solution to a problem is as plain as the hand in front of your face.

AQUARIUS: You might feel like you are weighed under by a particularly heavy load. Get help and make a clean start of it.

PISCES: Keep abreast of what's happening by calling a close relative every two hours.

doctor dolittle, m.d.

All the pediatricians I interviewed were naturally floored when I inquired about the availability of kennel boarding for the weekend.

But I kept getting confused. I had a lot of trouble not thinking of them as vets for hairless cats—after all, the initial visits with an infant are similar to the small pet checkup routine. The patient is carried in and has nothing to say. The physician listens to the heart and lungs, checks the ears for infections and parasites, throws the little animal on the scale, and gives it a few shots. Then the doctor exits, leaving you alone to wrestle the darn thing back into the box, or, in the case of the baby, back into its clothes.

For fifteen years I had been telling people about my cats' vet, so it just seemed natural to say, "I'm taking Kelly to the vet's today." And to compound the confusion, I ended up choosing a young female pediatrician who wants to be called by her first name, Bidi. My vet is a young woman named Beppy. Bidi and Beppy. Should these two be allowed to practice in the same city?

Maybe I set up the situation subconsciously to ease the transition into motherhood. Over at my vet's, I had already dropped thousands of dollars and generated sheafs of medical records for Sonny Crimmins, Minnie Crimmins, Monty Crimmins, Shlomo Crimmins, Cosmo Crimmins, Midgie Crimmins, Bubba Crimmins, Edie Crimmins, Eliza Crimmins, and Daisy Crimmins. Wouldn't it be easier if there were pediatric-veterinarian practices in which all of one's dependents could be cared for under one roof?

Eventually I got used to the idea that pediatricians *are* a bit different than vets—for one thing, they're more expensive, and they keep you waiting longer. Other differences:

- Pediatricians keep more inconvenient hours and don't even risk getting clawed (well, bitten, maybe).
- Pediatricians give stickers to reward their clients and have toys in their waiting room.
- Pediatricians do not teach you how to tilt your child's head back to throw a pill down her throat.
- Pediatricians know almost nothing about fleas and hairballs.

Immunizations I'd Like to See

Shots are an important part of the pediatric regimen for the first year of baby's life. But is the current repertoire of immunizations, designed to guard her against all those old musty diseases, really enough preparation for modern living? A few more possibilities:

Liberal Arts Repulsion (LAR) Shot. Given at three months of age, prevents your child from ever trying to make a living as a performance artist, painter, poet, or musician. A special booster shot one year later, MBA (Make Bucks Always), ensures a six-figure income.

Weasels Shot. Given at fourth year checkup. Protects your offspring from falling in with the wrong crowd in school and, later, at the office.

Delirium, Passion, Titillation (DPT). Administered at eight months, vaccinates child against future disappointing love affairs and boring dinner party conversations.

Folio Serum. Enables child to read original Shakespearean documents at age of two and get Hollywood backing for his or her own production of *Henry V* soon after kindergarten.

milestones of the first year

### 5–6 weeks	Smiles.

From this point on, baby will smile periodically, but never when a camera is present. Research shows that very young babies are acutely aware of their lack of teeth, so you can solve the photo-op problem by buying your newborn tiny dentures.

### 3–4 months	Rolls over.

When you leave the room, the baby's on her stomach, and then when you return she's on her back, snickering up her stretchie sleeve at the success of her first practical joke. But don't expect to entertain your friends with this exciting new trick. Babies won't roll over on command, no matter how many hours you stand over them with a handful of biscuits.

### 6–8 months	Sits up.

This usually happens at the same time that they learn to reach out and grab things. Babies at this age make excellent highway tollbooth collectors.

### 8–10 months	Crawls.

An important step in motor development—enables baby to further integrate herself into family life by sharing the cat's food and spitting up in clandestine locations.

9–12 months   Says first word.

Books report that "Daddy" is a popular favorite, with objects such as "hat" and "ball" following close behind. I missed this milestone. My baby would only utter her first word whenever I was out of the room—visitors thought it sounded like "help!"

12 months   Walks.

The lurching, stiff gait . . . the innocent clumsiness . . . the terribly destructive tendency to lay waste to everything in its path. Where have you seen it all before? On late-night horror movies, of course. The new toddler might be lovable, but at least Frankenstein was toilet-trained.

mommy nearest

Having your mother visit after you have a baby is a time-honored tradition in female culture. While many folks just assume that this custom arose because the new mom needs help, I know better. Your mom's presence with you all day long for weeks on end is nature's way of providing you with a focus of anxiety other than the new baby.

Face it—you worry that you'll never be half the mom your mother was, and then there she is in the flesh to prove it, cooking all your favorite childhood foods, doing the laundry, dusting your lampshades, and telling you fairy tales about how she and Dad never lived beyond their means.

This is the time when you are supposed to be initiated into the mysteries of motherhood, and yet the sheer competency of this woman intimidates you. You know that you'll never be able to do any of these mom things. You picture yourself years from now going to visit your daughter after *she* gives birth: what will you do, bring along a pizza, a six-pack, and a professional nurse?

I decided to cope with my overwhelming feelings of maternal inadequacy by having a minor nervous breakdown while my mom was there. Not for me this weepy stuff where you just mope around the house in a low-grade postpartum slump. No, I wanted something dramatic, something that would get my mommy's attention and make her stay forever to take care of me. (Could we find a double stroller that would fit me *and* the baby?)

Kelly was asleep, and my mother and I were sitting watching television, when suddenly I noticed strange shadows flitting across my field of vision.

"Don't be alarmed, Mom, but I think I'm having a cerebral hemorrhage. The whole room is going dark."

"Oh, honey—are you sure you're not just feeling a little faint? Why don't you just take a nap?"

"No! This is the big one! I always knew I would die in childbirth, and now it's happening."

"But dear—you had the baby four days ago."

"So I'm a little bit late. Please, call the doctor," I said, staggering into the bedroom.

An hour went by, and I was still alive and had managed to nurse the kid and eat a plate of crackers and cheese. But by the time a nurse midwife rang the bell and entered, I was once again languishing on the bed, seeing dots and stripes and imagining what I'd look like after major brain surgery.

"You're fine," chirped the nurse after taking my blood pressure. "I think it's just that your milk is coming in, and the fluid levels are a bit off in your body. That's why your vision seems strange. It will probably go away in a few hours."

My mother smiled knowingly, the way she used to when I would try to fake illnesses to get out of school. Slowly, I realized that there was no getting out of it this time—and the homework was going to be much worse, I could tell.

Handy Translation Guide

Do you have trouble communicating the unique abilities and needs of your baby to your mom? That's because she gave birth to an older-model baby. You have brought forth the new, improved model, and it shows each time you open your mouth. Here's a chart to help you and your mom find common verbal ground while discussing her grandchild.

New Model Baby (Yours)	Old Model (Mom's)
Communicates needs nonverbally	Cried
Tracks objects	Looked at things
Uses infant bathing center	Took a bath in the sink
Requires black and white stimulation center	Had a cute mobile
Has a father with nurturing role	Had a dad who paid bills
Attends playgroup	Went along with Mom to coffee klatsch
Has caregiver	Had a teenaged babysitter

the six-week postpartum checkup: am i feeling maternal yet?

1. My baby's cries are
   A. Easier to listen to than fingernails on a chalkboard.
   B. Important communications that predict fluctuations in the stock market.
   C. The most effective telephone solicitor repellent on the market.

2. I feed my baby
   A. When I feel like it.
   B. Every five sitcoms whether he needs it or not.
   C. According to an ancient formula of demand and ocean tide listings.

3. The proper way to hold a baby is
   A. By the scruff of the neck.
   B. From the drawstring end of its nightgown.
   C. Like a football that might throw up any minute.

4. The most important piece of equipment for the first few weeks of life is
   A. A stimulating crib mobile.
   B. A soothing lullaby tape.
   C. A gallon of Scotch and cable t.v.

5. If they made a movie of my life right now, it would be called
   A. Jaws 4.
   B. Curse of the Mommy's Womb.
   C. Night of the Living Dead.

6. I would like to have sex again
   A. With the diaper service man.
   B. Sometime in the twenty-first century.
   C. If I can use three or more contraceptive methods.

Scoring: If you are alert enough to want to take this test, go back to work or take up a time-consuming hobby. If you answered all the questions, go take a nap.

Late Night Revelations . . .

For all of our evolutionary advantages, do humans have this reproduction thing down wrong? In many of the lower organisms—plants, insects, most fish—you flower or spawn and then you croak off. You don't stick around to go to school pageants. Dying right after the young hatch just might be a savvy strategy practiced by the lower animal orders to avoid drudgery and diaper service bills.

---

the anti-mom approved list of toys for very small babies

Why support Fisher-Price when you can make do with things around the house? Save your money later for when your child knows the difference.

Rubber Rat or Snake (Approximately $2.95)
Can be purchased in any novelty store.
Advantages: Keeps little old ladies away from child in park.
Drawbacks: Slight chance that buzzard or other bird of prey will swoop down on baby. Advise using indoors.

Wine Cork (Free, at least if you were going to drink the wine anyway)
Advantages: You won't be able to recork the wine after the kid gets finished gumming the stopper, so you might as well drink it all.
Drawbacks: Once baby gets teeth, she can chew off small or large chunks of cork. However, this helps her float better in the bathtub.

Peppy La Pew Valentine's Day Card (Approximately $1.00)
Advantages: Strong black and white image for building of visual tracking skills.
Drawbacks: Might make child a hopeless Francophile and lifelong fan of Jerry Lewis movies.

Empty Plastic Aspirin Bottle (with cap removed) Free (but paid for with all your postpartum headaches)
Advantages: Sounds good when thrown on floor; subtly indoctrinates child into drug culture and makes up for all the aspirin you couldn't take while pregnant.
Drawbacks: Too big a toy to be shared with cats.

Perforated Computer Paper Edges ("After-Perf")
Free
Advantages: Recycling can help baby understand importance of saving Planet Earth.
Drawbacks: After ingesting massive amounts of wood pulp, child might boot up dinner.

SIPRESS

BABIES: An Illustrated Owner's Manual

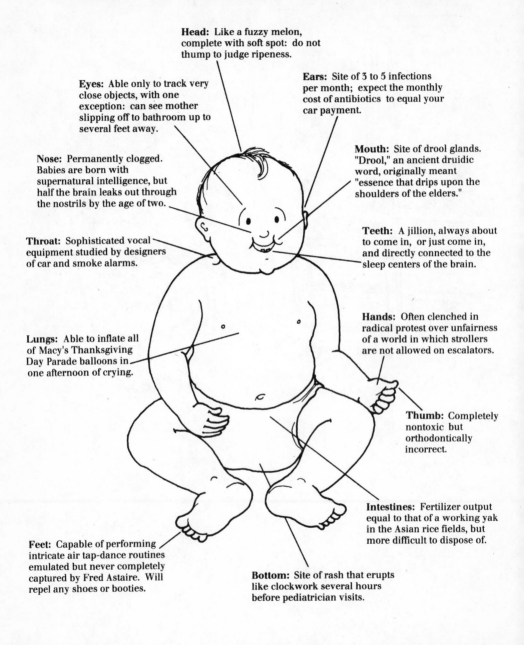

Head: Like a fuzzy melon, complete with soft spot: do not thump to judge ripeness.

Eyes: Able only to track very close objects, with one exception: can see mother slipping off to bathroom up to several feet away.

Ears: Site of 3 to 5 infections per month; expect the monthly cost of antibiotics to equal your car payment.

Nose: Permanently clogged. Babies are born with supernatural intelligence, but half the brain leaks out through the nostrils by the age of two.

Mouth: Site of drool glands. "Drool," an ancient druidic word, originally meant "essence that drips upon the shoulders of the elders."

Throat: Sophisticated vocal equipment studied by designers of car and smoke alarms.

Teeth: A jillion, always about to come in, or just come in, and directly connected to the sleep centers of the brain.

Hands: Often clenched in radical protest over unfairness of a world in which strollers are not allowed on escalators.

Lungs: Able to inflate all of Macy's Thanksgiving Day Parade balloons in one afternoon of crying.

Thumb: Completely nontoxic but orthodontically incorrect.

Intestines: Fertilizer output equal to that of a working yak in the Asian rice fields, but more difficult to dispose of.

Feet: Capable of performing intricate air tap-dance routines emulated but never completely captured by Fred Astaire. Will repel any shoes or booties.

Bottom: Site of rash that erupts like clockwork several hours before pediatrician visits.

the cotton scam

Wondering why your baby's layette is costing more than your first year's college tuition?

You have fallen prey to baby tog propagandists. You've begun thinking of your baby as a person who really cares what she wears, who has friends who will be asking her just where she got that delightful Christian Dior onesie.

But your kid can't see very far, can't talk, and certainly doesn't know that little Chloe-Elizabeth down the street only pee-pees into French diapers. This is your chance to ignore preconceptions about clothing class and status and save yourself a bundle. So when it comes to outfitting a brand-new, fairly brainless person, think nerd. Pickup-driving, beer-swilling, polyester-wearing nerd. (Well, you don't have to focus on the first two—just the polyester part.)

Admittedly, dressing your kid downscale will be hard to do in the face of all the beautifully photographed full-color catalogs you receive in the mail. I mean the ones with the bonnets designed by Nobel Prize winners and the 100% alpaca buntings that have been tested by mother-son mountain climbing teams in the Himalayas.

But just look at the tremendous savings—

shoppers—let's compare!!!

Hanna-May's Harvard-Bound Fashion Catalog. 100% cotton stretchie with NASA-designed closures. Comes with twenty-page biodegradable booklet detailing how each puff of cotton was individually harvested by Swedish obstetricians on holiday and then dyed by Hopi Indians into colors chosen to intellectually stimulate your newborn and enhance her self-esteem.
Price: $34.99

K-Mart 100% polyester stretchie. Delightful, pungent chemical aroma when you remove it from wrapper (diminishes with repeated washings), sophisticated visual motif of singing ducks or mice strengthened graphically in some versions with witty remarks emblazoned on the front of the garment such as "I Wuv Daddy." Available in muted tones of pink, yellow, and blue.
Price: $3.49

Eco-Kids Greenwear Catalog. Infant rain poncho made of natural rubber hand-collected by nonoppressed natives in approved Rain Forest villages, cooked in open pits which double as an energy source for several Latin American countries, and then gently dyed with the resin of brazil nut shells to a tawny, pleasing shade of brown. Toggle top closure with fake whale tooth carved of nonendangered mahogany bears the names of all the important pharmaceuticals discovered in the Rain Forest since 1948.
Price: $32.50

Any supermarket. Biodegradable plastic bag—self-cutting feature allows parent to fashion neck opening to desirable size; store logo in simple graphic style lends a sophisticated look. Special warning on bag reminds consumer that it is meant to be worn, not played with by children.
Price: Free

Go for the Better Baby Clothing Through Chemicals approach, and in each instance you've saved yourself a cool thirtysomething bucks— six hours of babysitting, one bottle of French champagne (so much more rewarding than French kiddie togs), or two tubes of ridiculously overpriced lipstick. And your kid's none the worse for wear.

stupid accessories for baby

Baby Monitor

Who was the demented walkie-talkie maven who decided that parents need to hear each little hiccup their kids make? How is a kid going to develop lung power if every little whimper makes Mom come running? My recommendation: Keep the baby monitor you got as a gift and put it under the guest bed—lots more fun!

Hanging Diaper Dispenser

Oh, right—can't wait to take those disposable diapers out of the plastic bag and put them, one by one, into something that looks like a clown or a duck. Right. And after that I'm going to iron all my baby's undershirts, too.

Baby Book

Living through baby's first moments is hard enough: writing about them is cruel and unusual punishment. Besides, those books filled with teddy bear illustrations never have entries for Baby's First Projectile Vomiting.

Front Strap-On Carriers

If guys want to wear babies strapped to their bellies, fine, but what is pregnancy if not an *internal Snugli*? Now that the kid has seen the light of day, I have no desire to create my own external protuberance. Let the man in my life learn to waddle.

Anti-Mom's Food Credos

It's never too early to learn liking sushi.

Pizza crusts make excellent teething biscuits.

I grew up eating white sugar, and it will do wonders for my kid, too.

If something has been on the floor less than four days, it is still edible.

If God had meant me to finish breadcrusts, he would have made me a sea gull.

---

ask anti-mom

Dear Anti-Mom,

Why do people have children?

> *Bothered and Bewildered at 2 A.M.*

Dear Bothered,

A national survey has found that people have children because of
 1. A desire to cut back on their sex lives (62%).
 2. Attraction to Velcro (25%).
 3. A wish to dispose of income without consulting insurance agents or bankers (13%).

Dear Anti-Mom,

How can I get my little one to sleep through the night? I haven't rested more than three hours consecutively for the last eighteen months.

> *REM-less and Red-eyed*

Dear REM-less,

You're asking me? My kid learned her numbers by watching David Letterman's Top Ten list. She recites infomercials on baldness remedies at her day care center.
 There is no cure for baby sleep dysfunction—only prevention. You must mate with a person with appropriate brain

waves and sleep chromosomes. My husband is forty and still doesn't sleep through the night—that should have told me something.

Dear Anti-Mom,

Can you recommend an effective remedy for teething problems?

Aching in Abilene

Dear Aching,

Old-fashioned remedies are best. Dip your finger in a glass of whiskey and massage your infant's gums. Then down the whiskey. Repeat if necessary—by the third time, you no longer have to apply the whiskey to the infant.

Things to Pass the Time When You Are Up in the Middle of the Night With Your Baby

- Call your high school sex education teacher
- Order yourself a $6,000 Hovercraft from the Hammacher Schlemmer catalog
- Make airline reservation for one to Paris
- Hear voices telling you to assassinate Demi Moore
- Call the hospital to see if there has been a baby recall for your model

white noise in the nursery

The books will tell you that each cry your baby makes means something different. In those first few important weeks of life, you begin to distinguish the cry that says, "I am hungry," the one that says, "I am sleepy," and the one that says, "I am worried about global warming."

But there is one cry that is off the chart as far as decibel level and intonation. It is the cry that says, "Hello, I am the worst-case scenario for new motherhood." That is the cry of the colicky baby.

Colic means hours of meaningless, stream-of-consciousness crying. No one knows what causes colic, but all your friends and relatives will have theories. If you're breastfeeding, it could be something you eat that irritates the baby. If you're bottlefeeding, doctors and busybodies will tell you to switch formulas.

Your baby might also have colic because you are high-strung, because she hates the new wallpaper in her room, or because she is the reincarnation of a little girl whose lollipop you stole in second grade.

Even if you knew conclusively that colic came from a special gland that later ensures a tranquil adolescence, it still won't take your mind off the incessant shrieking. Nothing does.

Kelly had two periods of high-pitched colic frolics each day, one at about four to seven P.M. and the other at one to three A.M. So I am an expert at failing to comfort a colicky infant. I walked three times around Earth's equator, rocked enough to wear a hole down to the subflooring, sang Kumbaya in jazz, rock, and rap versions, and tried a do-it-yourself exorcism kit.

I also tried giving her to Dad one weary night when I just couldn't jiggle, bounce, or rock anymore. He lasted about twenty minutes and then I heard him whispering in her ear, "I'm sorry, but I have to kill you now."

I rushed in and grabbed the child before he put all of us out of our misery.

It turned out that my incompetent housekeeping had kept us suffering far longer than necessary. One of the moms in the neighborhood casually mentioned that she had always turned on the vacuum cleaner to soothe her colicky baby. That afternoon, when the wailing commenced, I hauled out the canister vacuum cleaner that hadn't been used since I was two months pregnant. I turned it on, and—Eureka! Kelly shut her little mouth and dozed.

Of course, as soon as I turned the thing off, she woke up and started crying again. So for weeks we kept it on whenever she was fussy. That meant that we ate dinner with the vacuum cleaner on, watched television, and even slept as one very small spot of our floor became spic and span. Somehow, it never occurred to me that I could actually be vacuuming the floor while my baby slept, but it must have sounded like I had become possessed by the spirit of June Cleaver. My upstairs neighbor later said she thought that excess vacuuming was a sign of postpartum depression.

Eventually I weaned Kelly to a blender as a source of soothing white noise, and I was about to trade down to an electric leg shaver when the colic mysteriously departed, as all the books say it will by about three months of age. I never even got a chance to get rich on the invention I was working on, the baby-walker-vacuum cleaner.

If I Were Mother of the Universe . . .

All baby clothes and bibs would be black.
Children would not grow hair until the age of ten.
Baby's scalps would have Velcro inserts to keep hats on.

great anti-moms from other cultures

Every time I feel like I can't cope with the demands of motherhood, I think of the moms in the Hebei and Shandong provinces in northeastern China. These moms have devised an incredibly efficient form of day care. They keep their babies in sandbags.

Yes, sandbags, not sandboxes. Sometimes life is stranger than fiction.

A week after the babies are born, they are placed in bags filled with silt gathered along the banks of the Yellow River. Their little arms are left free, but they can't move their legs. According to reports, the silt makes an excellent kiddie litter, and the moms change it daily, so the babies never develop rashes. Okay, so the kids don't learn to walk until they're fourteen months, but the parents save on diapers, and they don't have to do any babyproofing. The moms work in the fields all day and then return at noon to nurse the babies, who stay in the sandbags about twenty hours a day.

So maybe I'm sick, comparing myself to parents in a third world culture with an average yearly income of $27. But sometimes you just need to think, when you've had one of those bad days, "Hey—I could have decided to keep you in a sandbag!" And sometimes, when you're headed out on one of those Sunday-afternoon jaunts with a trunk filled with fifty pounds of baby equipment, it's nice to daydream about how, in northern China, you could just grab your kid and some silt and head out the door.

babyproofing: some theories

Much is made of babyproofing these days. Parents can even hire babyproofing consultants to help them identify and eliminate potential hazards in their households.

I have two problems with the idea of conscious, large-scale baby-proofing operations.

1. **Will babyproofing tamper with evolution?**   Will we breed a race of adults who still touch the flame on a stove if not protected by a little metal railing? Will we see the development of full-body airbags required by law to be worn when awake? Would it change the course of human history if parents put rattlesnakes under the sink instead of a lock on the cabinet?

2. **Why is it that, no matter how much you babyproof, tykes will always find something potentially harmful around the house?**   My friend Sandy called me one day, hysterical. "I got rid of everything I could think of that was dangerous, and then I saw Matthew chewing on the *wall*. He even got a chip off it. He's going to be brain-damaged!"

Think about it: The only truly babyproofed house is one in which babies can't get into it at all but are kept in a separate kennel in another location until they develop common sense. Professional babyproofers should escalate their efforts, using historical models to provide the ultimate in comfort for anxious parents. The castle moat—now there's a good example of a possible babyproofing device. Or how about the padded prison cell?

baby p.r. tricks, or there's a sucker you're born to every minute

I try my best to maintain my cynicism, which is hard to do as a mother in the face of relentless cuteness. Actors have known for years not to play scenes with babies and dogs. Now, at last, I can expose the standard public relations strategies of babies so that, while still falling prey to their charms, we can recognize them for what they are: advertisements to keep you feeding and clothing them.

Eye Contact: The Baby P.R. handbook advises using this one early, and often, like any good salesman. Fortunately, new babies cannot yet repeat your name over and over while they are staring at you.

Smiling: Most adults fall for this every time. Infant public relations experts recommend developing a range of mouth movements, which can convince those special adults in your life that you have a unique smile in your repertoire just for them.

Googling: In this brilliant verbal strategy, babies take a page from the P.R. manual for cats, which notes the absolute success of making a constant, soothing sound for owners' ears.

Addiction: Nothing flatters like someone who bursts into tears the moment you leave the room and who chants your name over and over.

A Glimpse into the Future

It will come along too late for me, but I believe that one day technology will solve the child care problem. All parents will have access to Virtual Reality Day Care, a computerized, completely interactive experience for our progeny.

Virtual Reality Day Care. Imagine—a world in which, each morning, you'd strap your kid into a tiny helmet and tactile mittens and leave the room. Your baby then would experience a stimulating, educational day in the privacy of your own home, without leaving his crib.

You could choose between two programs, Very Good Child, and Brat from Hell. In the first, your perfect child would get a simulation of all the usual nursery school experiences: art projects, storytelling time, insipid songs, show and tell. In the second, your naturally obnoxious youngster could do all the bad things he can think of without ever getting hurt: play with matches, stand up in the backseat of automobiles, fall from high places, eat the contents of two or three theme character vitamin bottles, etc. He'd spend his day like some Looney Tune character, secure in the idea that nothing could bump him off.

Virtual Reality Day Care could end worries for millions of parents worldwide.

PART III
terror in tinytown

It walks, it talks, it breaks your toys, it monopolizes the
t.v. set . . . fun with preschoolers.

raising the proto-human

Lots of people make the mistake of thinking that children under the age of five are human beings. Sure, they walk upright and have television cereal commercials written for them. But don't let this mislead you. Preschool children occupy space on the evolutionary chart several notches below *Homo sapiens* adulthood, and do not pass even the most basic test of what makes an animal human.

1. *They do not use tools.* You might think they do, but try having someone fix your leaky faucet with a Fisher-Price plastic wrench or fill in your 1040 with crayons.
2. *They do not have a sophisticated symbol system.* Yes, they can recognize the McDonald's golden arches a half mile away and sing umpteen verses of "Little Rabbit Foo-Foo," but that doesn't count.
3. *They do not have a moral code.* In scientific experiments, two-year-olds and rats were put into a room filled with M&Ms. The two-year-olds eventually eliminated the rats and were starting on each other when researchers intervened.

Of course, there are some childrearing experts who will dispute these findings. But even they would be forced to agree that, among human life forms, small children are closer to Neanderthals than to modern man.

Say you were to invite a Neanderthal home. Chances are you would have to teach him how to use the toilet and to eat with a spoon and fork. You would have to keep him from making crayon drawings of bison on the walls of your house, and you might even have to lecture him about playing with matches.

I use the Neanderthal analogy often during times of parental stress. Here are some other useful ways of mentally distancing yourself and other normal humans from the preschool population.

They're not really toddlers, they're . . .

- tiny co-dependents
- time bombs with chocolate milk moustaches
- aliens from a planet with shabby toilet habits
- walking advertisements of your disposable income level
- lifetime bathroom companions
- human petri dishes for virus cultures
- descendants of mentally ill munchkins who came back with Dorothy
- consumer targets for fast-food chains
- acolytes in the Cult of the Dustbuster
- future readers of self-help books
- noisy illiterates
- public service reminders for birth control

finding the perfect project

If you were a good Girl Scout, you will make a good mom.

Unfortunately, I was a lousy scout. I especially hated camping trips. I didn't like getting my hands all yucky, or singing inane songs for hours, or eating overcooked hot dogs and soggy graham crackers. I especially hated any craft projects involving Clorox bottles or clothespins.

Being alone in a house with a toddler is like a Girl Scout camping trip where it rains every day, and Anti-Moms are not happy campers.

The books on childrearing talk about the need to play stimulating games and make your own Play-Doh and fingerpaints. What they don't tell you is that toddler attention spans vary wildly. At two, Kelly could concentrate on a finger painting project for about two to three minutes, but while I was making the paints, setting up the newspapers, and swathing myself in layers of protective plastic, she would spend the entire half hour carefully poking holes in the screen door with a screwdriver.

This happened over and over. I would start out the morning thinking, "Okay—let's do peek-a-boo!" and that would take up about ninety seconds. Next we'd move on to crayoning, which would sometimes eat up another four minutes. Then I'd get a phone call and when I got off discover that she had patiently spent eighteen minutes Scotch-taping Cheerios to the mahogany coffee table.

I began to think that the books were wrong. Maybe toddlers should plan their own projects. Maybe they inherently sense that making cutout snowflakes will not prepare them for their future lives, whereas flushing four pounds of marinated tuna steaks down the toilet will give them an overview of household plumbing and a rudimentary understanding of aquatic migration patterns.

Realizing the keen toddler desire for reality-based art projects, I began to look around for some. Mostly, I let Kelly be my guide in this. Scotch tape was nearly always the medium of choice. She would spend over an hour Scotch-taping my feet and legs together while I read a novel or talked on the phone. She was happy, and so was I. Wrapping my legs in sticky adhesive which she later ripped violently off prepared her for a future as a sadistic salon worker, and I got a leg-waxing job for the price of a roll of tape.

reality suzuki

Parents of preschoolers are familiar with the Suzuki method of teaching violin and cello on small-scale instruments. But is Suzuki violin a really useful skill for kids, or an especially pleasant experience for parents during practice time?

Try one of these other Suzuki mail order courses, and you'll get more for your money.

Suzuki Stockbroker   Teaches the principles of investment with special editions of the *Wall Street Journal* featuring the famous "Billy Bull and Betty Bear Go to Market" stories. In just a few weeks, your tiny financial advisor will be handling your portfolio like a pro.

Suzuki Sommelier   Your child learns colors—red, white—and numbers (1982, 1986) in this fabulous hands-on program, which also introduces him to the geography of France, Australia, California, and Italy. Includes a plastic faux champagne bucket and a safety corkscrew.

Suzuki Housekeeper   Help your child go beyond dustbusting with this comprehensive course put together by English maids and butlers. A new kind of potty training that will leave your bathroom in tiptop shape.

tips for taking toddlers to restaurants

Don't do it.

But you will. Like all zombies, you will find yourself returning to those places that used to be fun in your other life. Glazed and uncomprehending, you will not understand the horrified looks on the other restaurant patrons' faces, or why they run away to another section.

Sometimes, when babies are very small, going out to eat works okay. On a good day, when the moon is rising in Marsupia and the kid is conked out in her kangarockarockabooboo contraption, you'll be tempted to think that good family dining experiences lie ahead. This is a trick. Babies are programmed to allow you several good restaurant experiences, part of a diabolical plan to keep you from learning the truth too early: The human offspring has pizza priorities that must be met, and cannot be met in the types of places frequented by childless diners.

In the second phase of preparing you for an eternity of throwing out big white boxes, the small child springs into more direct action, using guidelines established by the Toddler Restaurant Commission.

Restaurant Guidelines for Those Under Three

1. If you are asleep when your parents enter the restaurant, allow them time to get seated and begin to think, "Wow—maybe he'll stay down." Then wake up, but not pleasantly. Cry and scream. Fight for your life on the off-chance that this could be a "pick your own baby" restaurant where you are the main course instead of a bunch of lobsters—you can never be too careful.

2. As soon as the food has arrived, take an enormous poop, the smell

and magnitude of which your parents and the diners at nearby tables cannot ignore. (Toilet-trained already? Ask to go to potty. Missing it or not making it on time adds a nice touch.)

3. Ignore any toys that your parents have thought to bring with them. Instead, insist on playing with car keys and losing them under a radiator, or whine until Mom gives you her wallet to dismantle, then throw the Visa card down an air-conditioning vent.

4. Every couple of times, remember to throw up on the waiter or waitress.

5. Don't hesitate to slip out of your parents' sight and eat all the maraschino cherries at the end of the bar, or crawl under a table and up an old lady's leg.

6. The little packets of sugar are left there for small children to open and dump on the floor or into their parents' entrees.

7. Feel free to make up inventive games that involve putting ice cubes all over the table.

8. Always leave more food on the floor around your place than on your plate.

9. Hide your security object or blanket, so that your parents will have to return to the restaurant several hours later and crawl all over on their hands and knees or sift through the dumpster.

10. Picking all the petals off flower arrangements is a nice way to let the staff know you care.

11. When things are getting dull, stroll among the tables performing "Itsy Bitsy Spider" or strip off all your clothes and do an interpretive dance.

For Parents: Some Things That Can Make You More Popular as You Leave a Restaurant

1. Leave a 50% tip.
2. Leave a pack of condoms.
3. Sign an affidavit specifying that you are moving to Kuala Lumpur and will never return again.

milestones of early childhood

Responds to Video (16 to 18 months)   The onset of television addiction begins only after child can stay still for more than one and a half minutes. The true signs of t.v. rapture—open mouth, direct, vacant stare at the screen—can be a very moving moment, pointing the way to new possibilities for showering and talking on the telephone.

Discovers Candy (anywhere from 12 months on)   Opens up a world of future dental adventures and increased energy. Prepares child for the next achievement.

Responds to Bribery (19 months on)   Nature knows what it is doing. Bribery responsiveness develops at about the same time the child decides never to cooperate with you again, but soon after child has learned that candy is worth capitulation.

Pays First False Compliment (25 months on)   Typical first line, "You're so beautiful, Mom." This Eddie Haskell behavior pattern is an important step in mental development: Your child, growing progressively less cute as she ages, realizes that verbal skills will now play an important role in self-preservation.

Becomes Obsessed with Genitals (15 months to end of life)   When Kelly was two and a half, she and Alan and I were in a motel swimming pool, and she made up a little song, which she sang at the top of her lungs: "Oh, I'm swimming from Mommy's vagina to Daddy's penis, Oh yes I am, from Daddy's penis, to Mommy's vagina." Catchy lyrics, huh? In that one moment our family's failure to dream up cute euphemisms for private parts was revealed to one and all. Don't let it happen to you.

Tells First Obnoxiously Repetitious Anecdote (17 months and up) Kelly's was a droll, amusing story about how her shoe fell into the river otter's cage at the zoo and the animal swam laps with it. In telling it, she cut to the quick and omitted the boring details that drag down adult narratives. "A-Da Shoe Swim Swim," was, I believe, her witty version, which she would repeat to anyone who entered the room.

Learns to Whine (36 months and on and on and on)   It takes the human vocal cords a few years to be able to produce a sound so like fingernails on Styrofoam. There is the cheap whine, which can be remedied by small trinkets at the checkout counter, or the more mature, vintage whine which addresses all the wrongs you've ever perpetrated upon the child.

Discovers Guilt (32 months till forever)   You will recognize the onset of this phase by key phrases: "Don't leave me, Mommy!" "You said you were coming early—what took so long?" "Ashley's mommy picks her up at one o'clock."

Discovers Other People's Cars (31 months)   My daughter began recognizing the difference between a Mercedes-Benz dashboard and our own Toyota at a very early age. She now periodically approaches the owners of Jaguars in parking lots and offers to go home with them.

Repeats Television Commercials (24 months on)   Always happens when you are at a house of the Sanctimonious Parents, whose kids are only allowed to watch PBS.

Dials First Long-Distance Number (26 months)   If you're lucky, it will be a sympathetic relative who doesn't live too far away. If you're not, a $3000 kiddie gymnastics center will arrive by van two weeks later.

Leaves Home (216 months)   Well, not exactly early childhood, but it always helps to have something to look forward to.

Hi, stinky doody head!

ask anti-mom

▷▷▷▷▷▷▷▷▷▷▷▷

Dear Anti-Mom,

I have been experiencing a lot of difficulty separating from my three-year-old. Any tips?

Anxious in Alabama

Dear Anxious,

A lot of my more maternal friends complain of separation anxiety. Perhaps the best cure is to think about all the ways in which you really are a separate person and not at all like a preschooler.

Here's my list, and I encourage you to make up your own.

Differences Between Me and a Three-Year-Old

- I can think of only one activity that, when it's over, I feel like saying, "Let's do it again!"
- I get bored after my fourth viewing of *Big Bird Goes to China.*
- I like my pizza hot.
- I can color inside the lines.
- I can control my natural urges to strip down naked and show my rear end to my husband's boss.

Dear Anti-Mom,

I get embarrassed when people see that my four-year-old is still sucking on a pacifier. Little old ladies come up to me in shopping malls and scold me for being a bad mother. What can I do?

Binkies Anonymous

Dear Binkies,

Yes, little children do persist with disgusting habits that make us look bad, don't they? That's why I've perfected my new over-the-counter line of ToddlerDerm skin patches. They treat these addictions invisibly, alleviating parental discomfort. The patches come decorated with cartoon characters—kids love 'em. Here's one that will solve your problem quickly, plus a few others for common yet embarrassingly childish behavior.

SuckerDerm—Placed on arm, patch completely eliminates child's addiction to thumb or pacifier sucking.

BlankieDerm—Made from an actual tiny patch of your child's security blanket affixed to a porous backing. Attaches to the tummy to dispense that safe feeling a kid craves. Now no one needs to see pathetically filthy fabric remnants dragged along the ground. And your tyke won't ever lose BlankieDerm!

DroolawayDerm—Special pink-colored patch is placed inside the throat to eliminate that Wet Look.

Dear Anti-Mom,

What do you think of elaborate and expensive children's birthday parties?

Broke in Brooklyn

Dear Broke,

Normally, I approve of them for other people's children, since they give you and your spouse a few hours off during a Saturday to have sex. However, I do worry about the escalation of these affairs. Will a child whose third birthday features a catered party with clowns and robotic dinosaurs at an interactive museum expect a trip around the world by the time he is eight?

I've learned to get creative. Don't get stuck on the usual expensive themes and locations. The theme of my kid's fourth birthday party was Infectious Diseases. We took her and a few of her friends to a hospital emergency room.

anti-mom nutritional guide

Any parent knows that the preschool body naturally craves two substances: white sugar and grease. But until recently, parents thought that toddlers also needed reasonable amounts of green vegetables, fruits, and protein. Now the special government agency OKEI (Okay, Eat It) has revised the toddler food groups to create the Toddler Food Pyramid, a more accurate assessment of a small child's nutritional needs. A child need only eat the foods toward the top of this pyramid once or twice a month. However, the bottom four rungs must be consumed daily, and, in some cases, hourly, for survival of child and parent.

Corn

Apple Juice

Chicken Nuggets

Pizza and Spaghetti

Ice Cream and Popsicles

French Fries, Potato Chips

Orange Soda, Grape Soda, Coca-Cola

Candy Candy Candy Gum Candy Candy Candy Candy

> **If my kid were the only one in the world . . . an Anti-Mom fantasy.**
>
> - I could pay whatever I wanted and still get plenty of babysitting applicants.
> - I could give her an old cream cheese box, and she would never know what the other kids got for Christmas.
> - I could let her wear disposable diapers until she was twenty and we wouldn't even fill up one landfill.

bedtime rituals

The essential mothering skill of getting a kid to go to sleep is not one of my talents. Let's just say that I'm not going gentle into that good nitey-nite.

I remember, before our kid arrived, participating in a meaningful bedtime ritual that involved two people and was very relaxing.

Now, I spend hours reading stories about caterpillars with eating disorders and singing "Where is Thumbkin?" in the vain hope that my insomniac child will begin to get drowsy.

The reference books talk a lot about developing a bedtime ritual that will ease your child's transition into dreamland and convey the clear message that the day is over. Unfortunately, no matter how elaborate the ritual, my kid doesn't get the message.

"She's like the monster in a horror movie, the one that you think is dead but pops up again," said my husband when Kelly was less than two and we had just finished crawling on our bellies out of her room so that she wouldn't sense us leaving. My friend Larry, who has tried to put Kelly to sleep, is a father of two who says he has never seen such sophisticated radar in a sleeping kid before. "The Israeli army could use her as a motion detector."

In the early days, Alan and I used to participate in Kelly's bedtime ritual equally. But a problem began to develop—the lullabies and repetitious books put Alan to sleep, but not Kelly. I would leave him on the floor of her room, where he would wake up at two in the morning, about two hours after Kelly had finally gone to sleep.

I decided that literature and music were far too stimulating for our gifted child. Maybe the suspenseful twists in the plot line of *The Little Engine That Could* were keeping her awake. Perhaps she was puzzling over Freudian imagery in the lyrics of "Wynken, Blynken, and Nod."

She needed to be a video vegetable in order to fall asleep. I showed her a tape of Big Bird going to sleep and singing songs about going to sleep. This technique worked really well for me. After the third time through it, I began daydreaming about how many down pillows I could stuff with Big Bird. Then, before I knew it, I'd drifted off, awakening later to a t.v. test pattern and a child asleep on the couch.

children's books: some unanswered questions

Good Night, Moon

Who was eating that bowlful of mush? Is it left over from a Three Bears story? Does the little old lady have some connection to the story, or did she just wander in from the street to get warm?

Winnie the Pooh

Why is Eeyore so depressed? Shouldn't he be on medication? Is Piglet suffering from an obsessive-compulsive cleanliness fetish?

Stuart Little

Is Stuart's problem hereditary or a random genetic mutation? Did his mother eat too much cheese when she was pregnant?

Alice in Wonderland

Is falling down a rabbit hole just a cheap day care substitute for Alice's mother? Shouldn't she have babyproofed all the holes on her property?

Curious George

Is George a latchkey child? Has the Man in the Yellow Hat ever gotten legal custody of him?

Lowly Worm

Why does a worm need to wear a sneaker? Is it a sneaker from the left or right foot? What does he do with the other one?

Madeline

Didn't Madeline's parents check out the teacher/student ratio in her school before enrolling her? Where are they, anyway, cavorting on the Riviera?

bathtime

If cleanliness is next to godliness, then my kid is Satan's handmaiden. Fortune-tellers have been known to read the stains on her face. The dirt under her fingernails could sustain the vegetable crop for a family of four.

Summer is Kelly's only clean season because she goes swimming almost every day. Pool chlorine destroys all sorts of bad things on her skin surface, including any germs living in the Popsicle and Tootsie Roll deposits.

Sure, there are drawbacks. By the end of the summer, I notice that she's whiter and brighter and smells perpetually like Mr. Tidy Bowl's aquatic environment. Yet by winter I would give anything to have a thoroughly chlorinated child.

In winter, she passes through three distinct stages:

Clean
Sort of Clean
Smells Like a Lion's Cage

When she reaches the last phase, the fun begins. The water puppy who can swim without a tube is suddenly terrified of two feet of soapy bathtub water. We try fun approaches, evoking all the pop culture water imagery we can manage—Ernie's rubber duck, the Little Mermaid, or, my personal favorite, The Incredible Mr. Limpet. Then we try wheedling, bribery, and threats. Finally there's nothing for it but to dunk her, screaming, or decide to ignore the whole problem for another few weeks and sprinkle a lot of baby powder on her.

Kelly's teacher told me the other day that I simply *must* attend to my child's appearance. Her exact words were: "She looks like an orphan." I don't think that's true at all. Orphans are wards of the state. They are forced by law to take baths and comb their hair.

My Solutions to Childhood Grooming Problems

Problem	Solution
Won't comb hair.	Shave head, leaving silhouette of teddy bear with clenched fist.
Teacher complains of stains on child's hands.	Tell her they are unusual birthmarks.
Won't wear clothes.	Hire Demi Moore's body paint artist to paint Oshkosh outfit on naked child in indelible ink.

ANTI-MOM ARCHITECTURE: The Dream House

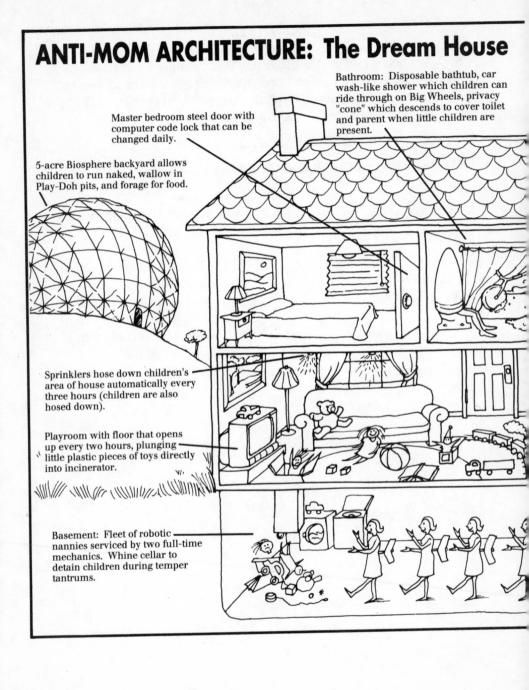

Bathroom: Disposable bathtub, car wash-like shower which children can ride through on Big Wheels, privacy "cone" which descends to cover toilet and parent when little children are present.

Master bedroom steel door with computer code lock that can be changed daily.

5-acre Biosphere backyard allows children to run naked, wallow in Play-Doh pits, and forage for food.

Sprinklers hose down children's area of house automatically every three hours (children are also hosed down).

Playroom with floor that opens up every two hours, plunging little plastic pieces of toys directly into incinerator.

Basement: Fleet of robotic nannies serviced by two full-time mechanics. Whine cellar to detain children during temper tantrums.

6-mile driveway with automatic car that can put children to sleep.

Soundproof wall down middle of house, children stay on one side.

Closets full of giant poncho-like garments that come out automatically on overhead wire and slip over children's heads without a hassle.

Library full of children's books that self-destruct after third reading.

One-way mirror across the wall — kids see you, you don't see them.

Phone automatically screens for any calls about volunteering at school; switches them over to 900 phone-sex line.

Own landfill out back to dump disposable diapers.

Microwave-fax machine that allows Grandma to send homecooked dinners for special occasions.

school days

What did I know about schools? When Kelly was eighteen months old, I didn't know the Montessori method from the Moe, Larry, and Curly method. I thought gross motor skills meant playing with your own feces.

I knew, though, that I would try to send my kid to a cute place two blocks down the street. It was convenient, seemed reputable, and I had already seen the inmates being led chain gang style on a rope down to the playground, so I knew they believed in fresh air.

The first time, Kelly and I missed the interview, which established my reputation as a conscientious mother. When we actually did make the interview, I can't say that it was particularly strenuous. What do you ask an eighteen-month-old—"Where do you see yourself in five years?"

The thing I remember most was the director's overwhelming need to convince me that parents were very involved with the school. That really scared the crap out of me. I didn't want anything to do with the school. Why would I want to spend thousands of dollars a year and still have to scrub down toys, or bake cupcakes? I didn't realize that having a child was going to mean sixteen years of committee projects. There should be a special, higher fee for those who can't handle that hearty sense of community. (Is cheerful volunteerism another hormonal side effect of motherhood that I escaped?)

Now that Kelly is in her third year of preschool, I've developed a checklist for Anti-Moms like me who are looking for schools.

- Ask about cultural diversity. The more culturally diverse a school claims to be, the more days off your kid will have while they celebrate all that stuff, and the more babysitting you'll need.

- Find out if the teachers and directors will replace the forms they send out at least twenty times without yelling at you.

- Subtly probe into how supportive they are of working mothers: for example, would they be upset if your kid got chicken pox and you sent her to school covered with Clearasil?

- Ask how many of the teachers babysit after school, and how many would be willing to dress and pick up your child in the morning.

- Get an estimate of the number of cupcakes you will be responsible for right up front, and see if you can bargain them down with rolls of toilet paper, old magazines, or troll dolls.

All-Purpose Phrasebook for School Volunteering Calls

"Darn, I'd love to help, but I just can't shake this case of leprosy I've had all winter."

"Yes, I can help. I would be able to bring a stick of butter."

"I don't know any child by that name."

artistic license

My kid is now producing about 750 drawings and paintings a year. I never know what any of them are (the last one, I thought, was a cat, but she swears it's a swimming pool). I don't care too much about content, but I'm concerned about the volume. I tell her she's going to saturate the market, but she won't listen.

Toulouse-Lautrec's mommy kept all his art projects. I know, because I saw the museum they fill in Southern France.

But Toulouse didn't start going to nursery school at age eighteen months, and I don't think, being French, that he was encouraged to trace his hand three or four times a day to create pictures of turkeys.

How much of this stuff am I supposed to save? I deposit most of it in the circular file. Am I foolish not to be building Kelly's portfolio so that someday there can be a one-woman retrospective in SoHo, "Kelly: The Early Stick Figures and Cotton Puff Collages"?

One mother at school told me that she had decided to withdraw her son and enroll him in a school with a much better art program. What kind of art program does she expect for someone with the motor skills of a squirrel monkey? I know that I wasn't producing masterpieces at two—I was spending most of my time sitting in supermarket carts and driving around in the back of my mother's car. And then, when I finally got to kindergarten, I created the first in a series of ashtrays, politically incorrect as art projects nowadays.

No one should call the stuff children produce art, unless they can convince me that real artists work in mediums like paper plates and tongue depressors. Parents should call this stuff what it really is: mess. When checking out schools, they should look for particularly good mess programs, because that's the real reason we're all so eager to have children do art projects at school—anything that keeps that glitter dropping on someone else's floorboards.

new movie suggestions for children

I don't think the people who make movies for children have even begun to cash in on some of the better ideas. Here are some genres they might want to try.

BIOGRAPHY: Raffi stars in *Young Gandhi*, a musical treatment of the early years of toddler hero Mahatma Gandhi. Song and dance numbers show how even as a youngster Gandhi was a natural at passive resistance: "No, no, I won't put on my sandals today," and, "You're gonna be sorry if you don't buy me that sari."

PRISON MOVIES: Big Bird in *Bird of Alcatraz*. The beloved Sesame Street character gets framed for the murder of a singing banana and becomes a legal scholar behind bars.

COMING OF AGE: *Little Mermaid Visits the Blue Lagoon*—the perfect opportunity for the Disney folks to combine fantasy with solid sex education.

HORROR/SUSPENSE: Barney the Dinosaur stars in *Jurassic Park II*, a futuristic thriller set on an island of incredibly friendly robotic dinosaurs who literally bore people to death. Horrible scenes include Barney singing the same song over and over until his victims drop.

the road to hell is paved with good nintendo

What is life? What is death? Is Chuck E. Cheese a messenger of Satan? Is Hell a steady diet of Chicken McNuggets without sauce?

I have a terrible recurrent nightmare: I'm taking an eternal road trip with my kid, and the only pit stops are kiddie attractions.

The nightmare starts like many of my normal waking experiences: I strap her into the car seat, and she announces that she has to go potty. We go into the house and come back, and I strap her into the seat again, but this time she's forgotten her security pillow. Another delay, and we're finally off.

We pull out of the driveway and go around the block, hitting an enormous traffic jam. We sing "Bingo" twenty-seven times, and she throws her Glinda the Good Witch figurine under the seat and asks me to get it. When I explain that I can't, she begins crying, and I offer her Tootsie Rolls. She eats nine of them, and then she throws up.

I know I have to get off the highway, but the places at the side of the road look unfamiliar. I turn into the first driveway, and the real scary part of the nightmare begins.

It's a giant toy department store. Kelly and I set off to find the rest room, but first we must navigate the concentric rings of Parent Hell. The place is set up like Dante's Inferno, with the most diabolical toys such as the $500 tiny Mercedes-Benz go-carts at the centermost depths of the store. Working our way around, we pass aisles of plastic pachyderms with neon hair, SWAT commando turtles, and dolls that fart, sing, and have sex-change operations. No bathrooms in sight, but there are at least 50,000 varieties of diapers available, coded to gender, weight, height, and zip code. Kelly, festooned with squiggles of Play-Doh that she has been shooting out of an extruder gun, is trying to talk me into buying her a computerized makeup table that doubles as a baby doll stroller when suddenly the scene dissolves, and we are back in the car again.

The car seems to be on automatic pilot now. We are on some weird ride in DisneyHades. We pull directly into a fast-food restaurant, where Kelly strips off all her clothes and jumps directly into the biggest vat of plastic balls I have ever seen. I cannot find her, and the only solution seems to be to get rid of the balls. An army of smaller toddlers is slowly eating the balls, making small choking noises that their mothers seem to ignore. I am about to start crying when . . .

Poof! Our car is on the road again, with the radio tuned to an all-Raffi station. Suddenly I realize that it's not a car at all, but an auto simulator at a family entertainment center. Kelly bolts out of her car seat, taking my watch with her to hock at the exchange counter, where she gets enough quarters to play Nintendo games for five hours.

I wake up in a cold sweat after about the fourth hour. My watch is gone from the bedside table. I go to Kelly's room, where she is fast asleep, clutching a quarter in one hand.

when does memory begin? a look at meaningful events

Should you take your kid to all sorts of stimulating cultural events, or should you leave her in a dark closet for the first three years of life? Psychologists have been debating this very issue for years.

Here's one certainty: The closet is cheaper. Take a look at what those golden non-memories add up to.

Cultural Events	*What They Remember*
Day at the Circus—Lithuanian jugglers, Romanian acrobats, East German mimes, ecologically correct animal acts. Total cost (including tickets, Sno-Kones flashlights, and other souvenirs: $112)	The elephant took a poop
2nd Birthday Party with Magician and Personalized Favors (Total cost, including wine and cheese for parents: $300)	The red balloon (19 cents)
Folk concert featuring PBS morning stars and a troupe of Spanish flamenco dancers (Total cost, including tickets and Happy Meals afterwards: $55.00)	Boy sitting next to us farted real loud.

Cultural Events
Ice Capades featuring Barbie on skates and Olympic-medal-winning performers (Tickets and Sno-Kones: $62.00)

What They Remember
On the way home the policeman stopped us and Mommy was going too fast and she got a ticket only it was different than the ticket she let me hold at the show.

Now sweetheart, you know it's not very grown up to spill your ice cream all over the couch and it's not nice to leave toys everywhere so that I have to pick them up...

blah blah blah blahty blah blah 'ice cream' blah blah blah blahty blahty blah blah 'toys' blah blah...

SIPRESS

holidays, from the grouchy mom's point of view

Remember when holidays used to be fun (and when the idea of a school vacation didn't strike you with dread)? That was B.C.—Before Cupcakes. Once you have produced a child, you are also expected to bake cupcakes for every sorry calendar celebration.

Mother's Day

A glimpse into unenlightened times, when Mother was given off one day a year for good behavior. Could she go out on the town, maybe see a movie, take in a show, flirt with GIs at a sleazy bar?

NOOOOOOOOO!

Her day off started as she was awakened by kids covered in batter thrusting a tray of charred discs onto her lap. Next on her fabulous fantasy agenda was the opening of an array of gifts crafted from Popsicle sticks and dried macaroni bits.

Then, time spent with the family for a change—going to church, perhaps, or looking at a local garden. If she was a really good girl, her family might take her out to dinner, or be extra nice to her while *she* cooked dinner.

Well, those were the days, back before mothers really asserted themselves. Why, Mother's Day is completely different now—isn't it?

Halloween

A fine American tradition of teaching our children to beg door to door dressed as mass murderers and co-dependent women. The planning takes weeks, but it's worth it just to see how lively a four-year-old can get after mainlining Milk Duds for three hours.

Thanksgiving

It is national law that moms must cook a turkey weighing at least three times more than the last baby they delivered. The labor for the meal must also take the same amount of time as actual childbirth, but the husband does not have to be present.

Christmas

(Founded by God's mom, who started the tradition of doing all the work for the holiday)

Moms shop, bake, lick stamps, make pageant costumes, wrap presents, tip mailmen, brave store lines, supervise the construction of endless chains of red and green rings, and collapse.

On the actual morning, a strange man gets all the credit, and moms receive stretch gloves and Dustbusters.

Valentine's Day

B.C.: An erotic holiday in which you were feted with flowers and candy. After: ceremonies focusing on doilies, construction paper, and the stuffing of cartoon character cards into thimble-size envelopes.

Easter

In a cruel homage to fertility, moms must boil dozens of eggs and participate in a group delusion that a giant rabbit delivers baskets filled with enough white sugar to keep the children of America hyperactive for three months.

Some False Messages About Parenthood from Your Television Set

- Parents who do not buy Volvos are endangering their children's lives.
- The stains on children's clothing can actually be gotten out.
- Men in clown suits and hamburger outfits will always be present to keep your children from whining during mealtimes.
- Airline flight attendants enjoy shepherding children to Disney World.
- Children take an intense interest in their parents' choice of breakfast cereals.

life can be lousy

Nitpicking detail. Can you really appreciate the phrase until your kid gets head lice?

The nursery school sends out a little flyer telling you

A. that head lice are totally natural and nothing to be ashamed of; and
B. that they don't want to see your disgusting kid again until you get rid of all the creepy crawly things on her noggin.

The flyer goes on to describe in glorious detail the life cycle of the head louse, which is kind of fascinating, like a Nova special. But then the prose turns downright nasty as it tells you how to exterminate the critters. This involves washing the kid's head and your own head with poison (they don't make Kermit the Frog head-lice shampoo), boiling the bedding, and exiling all comforting stuffed animals to the basement in sealed plastic bags.

Only then do you get down to the nitpicking stuff. Nits are the whitish eggs that stick to the scalp. They have to be picked off by hand or with these special little flea combs that come with the poison shampoo. If you don't pick off the nits, the things hatch and populate your follicles all over again.

Alan decided that this nit stuff could be a real occasion for family fun—why, we could all pick each other's nits, sort of like chimpanzees in the wild. I don't know—maybe I wasn't as much of a Jane Goodall fan. Maybe my jungle instincts are even less developed than my maternal ones. Anyhow, I balked at the whole idea of group simian grooming. As the smallest monkey howled for her stuffed teddy bear, Dad accused me of being uptight. I poured myself a drink and wondered if I could get my hairstylist to pick my nits—everyone should take responsibility for her own insect eggs, I reasoned, or pay somebody thirty-five dollars to do it.

Meanwhile, Alan—who is blessed with accountant's genes and never shies away from detail work—was running around the room trying to pick Kelly's head, giving up only after she wrapped a tablecloth around her skull and crawled under the dining room table.

The booklet came in handy again about seven days later when we witnessed the miracle of louse birth—it was better than an ant farm, or sea monkeys. And it gave us another chance to saunter over proudly to the local drugstore and let our child proclaim, "We need the shampoo for people with bugs in their hair!"

hit list of most annoying toy categories

1. *Legos and other tiny plastic things.* Billed as educational, they are actually just snap-together landfill candidates.
2. *Play-Doh.* Sterilized boogers in little cans convenient for eating or strewing around.
3. *Musical instruments and other noisemakers.* Should be set at outrageously high frequencies so kids could torture other species.
4. *Paints and Markers.* Liquids that can't be contained by diapers or toilets are big trouble.
5. *Games.* Will I get stuck in the sticky goo at Candyland? Will I be able to find the letters to spell "Cat" for Junior Boggle? Will we ever find all the pieces to put back into the box? The suspense is killing me.

unidentified moneyed objects

Soon Kelly will lose a tooth, and of course, in America, this milestone means yet another consumer opportunity. One of those "Morons R Us" catalogs offers a special tooth fairy pouch with your kid's name monogrammed on it. Only $14.95. The old under-the-pillow routine just doesn't cut it anymore.

In these days of safety consciousness, I'm surprised kids are even allowed to go around with loose teeth dangling. Shouldn't they be fitted with some sort of mouthguard to prevent accidental tooth swallowing, or shown an educational video about coping with tooth loss? And why is that nocturnal fairy still not subject to FAA, FDA, or EPA regulation?

Why the Tooth Fairy Should Be Regulated

- It makes unchaperoned visits to children late at night (and what gender is that tooth fairy, anyway?)
- It fails to fully disclose its tooth disposal site (Some third world country? Open ocean tooth-dumping?)
- It leaves small coins that could easily be swallowed.

performance anxiety

I like to heckle the performers at children's concerts because most of them are really atrocious. They think the kids don't notice how bad they are, and for the most part, they're right. Children have no taste. Anyone who has seen a Beauty and the Beast raincoat could tell you that. So being an "acclaimed" children's entertainer is nothing to brag about.

A folksinger comes to Kelly's school once a month. Kelly used to vomit every time he appeared. One of the teachers asked me if I could think of any reason why Kelly would cry really hard and throw up whenever this guy came to sing. I said that her father and I were also allergic to children's entertainers: maybe it's genetic.

But, alas, my kid outgrew this wonderful phase which made me believe she might have an aesthetic sense well beyond her years. She actually began to like this guy, and one day I had to take her to one of his concerts. Now it was my turn to feel sick to my stomach.

As much as I hate the singers, the puppeteers are worse. I remember one woman in Boston who had a real clever patter going—she would ask the kids which was the puppet, her or this pathetic piece of foam rubber. So I kept yelling, "You—it's you." But the kids, simpletons that they are, just loved answering correctly.

When did this vogue for children's entertainment begin? Is the baby boomer generation really so pathetic that we can't sing to our own children, or tell them stupid stories for free, rather than attending "Storytelling Festivals" for $10.95 a head?

Speaking as someone whose house is a Raffi-free zone, I think that parents are willing to fork over this dough for shoddy performances because they envy the lives of the performers, who don't have to go to an office every day. By supporting these aging hippies, parents can connect again to the days when they considered making a living strumming a guitar. And the performers can brainwash the children into harassing their parents about recycling and other hot topics.

So don't patronize these mediocre halfwits when anyone could do it. Use this list to go out there and do it yourself.

How to Become a Children's Performer: A Few Suggestions

- Discard your last name and grow a beard.
- Begin talking to your own hand in public places.
- Listen to old Harry Belafonte and Bing Crosby albums for inspiration.
- Begin to hallucinate that you can travel by tiny means of transportation into worlds with talking platypuses.
- Have cosmetic surgery to make you look like you're perpetually smiling.

Im sorry, sweetheart, but if Mommy has to listen to the music from "We Sing in Sillyville" one more time she'll lose her mind and then you won't have anybody to rent you any videos at all!

SIPRESS

Children's Performers Invade the Tabloids

They're on your t.v., they're on the tape deck of your stereo. They make full-length motion pictures. Someday soon you'll open up that *National Enquirer* or *World News*, and there they'll be:

Big Bird and Bigfoot Found in Love Nest

Sharon, Bram, and Lois Are Surviving Dionne Quintuplets!

**Shari Lewis Has Hushpuppy's Baby:
"And I'm Happy, Doggone it"**

**Mister Rogers Says, "Elvis Sighted in the Neighborhood,
gave Mr. Feeley Autograph"**

a cold of my own

As I look back on the first several years of motherhood, I realize my profound prepartum ignorance. I didn't know having a baby meant that I would probably never go to the bathroom alone again, or that all my "free" time would now cost at least five dollars an hour.

But the cruelest thing of all, the thing I still can't accept, is that I will never again have a cold of my own.

Every time I get a cold, Kelly already has one. And then Al gets it, and it's worse than mine. I never get a chance to revel in the ravages of a virus. No more watching bad sitcoms for hours or reading beach novels. No more sleeping for hours and then waking up and crying at fifties tearjerkers on the late show.

The best Mother's Day present anyone could give me would be a Flu and Cold Hideaway Weekend. Shoot me up with some nasty viral infection and send me off to a motel for three days with four boxes of tissues and a case of ginger ale. I would love it.

a promising future for anti-moms?
possible proof that cynicism is hereditary

Weeks before Thanksgiving, Kelly and I were watching *Sesame Street* and I grumbled (I thought under my breath) that someone should cook and stuff that Big Bird.

Thanksgiving morning, she asked me where the turkey was, and I told her it was still in the refrigerator.

"Is it Big Bird?" she asked.

"No, of course not."

"Awwww. I wanted you to cook Big Bird."

"You didn't really, did you? Wouldn't you be sad if I cooked Big Bird?" Her eyes narrowed and she looked at me severely.

"Cook 'im, Mom. Cook Big Bird, and for dessert, cook Cookie Monster, too!"

It was a holiday moment that warmed the cockles of my Anti-Mom heart.

About the Author

Cathy Crimmins is the author of seven books, including the bestselling *Official YAP Handbook, Entre-Chic: The Mega-Guide to Entrepreneurial Excellence*, and *The Secret World of Men*. Her articles have appeared in *Redbook, Savvy, Working Woman, The Village Voice, Working Mother*, and numerous other national publications.

A former standup comedienne, she has appeared on hundreds of radio and television shows nationwide. For several years she was a regular commentator for an NPR affiliate in Philadelphia and is currently developing a woman's show on the same station. She also serves as a creative consultant to numerous science museums across the country.

She lives in Philadelphia with her long-suffering husband and preschool daughter, Kelly, the guinea pig in the Anti-Mom experiment.